THE POINT OF IT ALL
Essays on Jesus Christ

BT
103
O54
2000

THE POINT OF IT ALL
ESSAYS ON JESUS CHRIST

J.C. O'NEILL

LEIDEN

Theological Seminar series, 1

ISSN 1566-2098

Copyright © 2000 Deo Publishing

Published by Deo Publishing
Scholeksterstraat 16, 2352 EE Leiderdorp, The Netherlands.

All rights reserved. No part of this publication may be reproduced, translated, stored in a retrieval system, or transmitted in any form or by any means, electronic, mechanical, photocopying, recording or otherwise, without prior written permission from the publisher.

British Library Cataloguing-in-Publication data
A catalogue record for this book is available from the British Library

NUGI 632

ISBN 90 5854 005 7

Contents

Preface vii

1. The Bankrupt Atheism of Modern Thought 1
2. Barth on the Heart of the Matter 17
3. What Would the Messiah Be Like? 27
4. Jesus' Messianic Awareness 73
5. The Parables of Jesus 97
6. The Events around the Birth and Resurrection 117
7. Why is the New Testament Doctrine of the Death
   of Christ So Elusive? 127
8. The Point of Christology 138

Bibliography..151

Preface

It is now about two thousand years since Jesus Christ was born. The point of it all is to remember this with gratitude. Thinking people in the Western world have been largely robbed of the point. The purpose of these essays is to help restore to them their heritage.

In the first chapter I argue that the widespread assumption that educated people can no longer believe in God is based on irrational and superseded arguments. In the second chapter, the sad fact is noted that some Christian theologians have been convinced by these arguments; I discuss the case of Karl Barth.

In the chapter I set out evidence for believing that many Jews before Jesus was born were expecting the incarnation of the Son of God and had seen the possibility that the incarnate Son of God would have to die. I hope to help the reader to understand that the great event celebrated every Christmas was not an arbitrary new happening that supposedly overturned all previous religious aspirations. If Anna the prophetess, or John the Baptist could look forward to a Messiah and Saviour, we too can recover some of their sense of expectancy as we look back. The third chapter is much longer than any of the others because it is necessary to give a detailed reply to a number of authoritative studies that try to show that messianic expectation among Jews at this time was neither important nor coherent. In reply, I attempt to show that this misreading of the evidence rests on a profound misunderstanding of how a religion works.

In the fourth chapter I argue that Jesus knew that he was the Messiah the Son of God—but also that he was forbidden by Jewish law to say so. This explains the widespread view of scholars that Jesus did not think he was the Messiah; they are relying on his silence about this point, but I argue that this silence was only to be expected. If Jesus had not thought he was the Messiah, the Son of God, it would be hard for his followers to adopt these beliefs. Since he did think this, the possibility is still open for people today to accept that he was who he thought he was, and who Christians ever since have thought him.

In the fifth chapter I show that the parables of Jesus were designed to help his listeners to prepare for the coming of the Kingdom of God, the time at the end of history when everyone would have to answer for their lives before the Messiah.

In the sixth chapter I examine the events surrounding Jesus' death and resurrection and argue that the evidence presented in the New Testament is not to be brushed aside.

In the seventh chapter I attempt to explain why there is so little connected teaching in the New Testament about the meaning of the death of Christ and to show what was likely to have been the agreed set of beliefs about that death.

In the final chapter I challenge the view that Paul taught that to be a Christian was to be in Christ, as though Christ was like the air in which plants breathe or the soil in which their roots are set.

The essays have been written and revised over many years, and I am grateful to those who asked me to speak to them or who accepted my offer of a paper for a seminar. I thank especially Stephen Priest who convened the Staff/Graduate Seminar of the Department of Philosophy in the University of Edinburgh at which the first chapter was read as a paper in February 1999, and Alanna Nobbs who invited me to give a lecture to the May 1997 annual conference of the Society for the Study of Early Christianity, Macquarie University, New South Wales, Australia, in preparation for which I wrote the third chapter.

I cannot argue anyone into faith, but I hope to be able to remove some obstacles for thoughtful people who would like to see the point of it all, and who find themselves strangely drawn to celebrating the birth of Jesus as a gift from God.

1

The Bankrupt Atheism of Modern Thought

There are certain key moves that have become almost axiomatic in educated circles. These key moves, if successful, ultimately rule out the existence of God. I shall try to set out these axioms as clearly and sympathetically as possible in order to reveal their unreasonableness. I shall challenge the assumption that there are no sound proofs of the existence of God. Finally, I shall argue that even the notorious problem of evil, which seems to show that God cannot exist because a moral God would not allow the evil we see all around us, is based on a premise which should count in favour of his existence rather than against.

What are the Roots of Modern Atheism?

It is still a moot question whether the great Scottish philosopher David Hume (1711–1776) was an atheist. Perhaps he was too much of a sceptic to be an atheist.[1] At least it can be said that the subtle and persistent objections that he gave Philo to deploy against the arguments of the two orthodox Christians, played, in his *Dialogues concerning Natural Religion*, by Demea the mystic and Cleanthes the rationalist, have made it very difficult for thoughtful thinkers ever since to be at ease with any of the usual ways of worshipping God. Immanuel Kant (1724–1804), upon whose thinking Hume had a decisive influence, postulated the existence of God, but upon such terms that belief in a God whose Son was born a human being was rendered almost impossible. Modern philosophers who follow Hume and Kant are usually out-and-out atheists.

---

[1] This is one of Richard Wollheim's three suggestions in support of his conclusion that "Hume never called himself an atheist, nor thought of himself as one." Wollheim (1963), pp. 28-30. For the view that he was an atheist and a discussion of his views on religion see Stephen Priest (1990), pp. 161-66.

I shall try to show that there are two axioms upon which this whole system of thought rests, both of which are unlikely to be true.

The first axiom is that it is unreasonable to take what Hume called "this little agitation of the brain which we call *thought*" as a model of the whole universe (Dialogue, Part II).[2] I shall argue that it is precisely this human ability that we do, entirely reasonably, take as a model for the whole universe when we see the universe as the creation of God.

The second axiom has two parts: first, there is no chance (Dialogue, Part VI, end; Part X;[3] and secondly, human free will and determinism are compatible (Kant's Third Antinomy [B 471-479; A 443-451]). Since the operation of most of the processes of modern technology is built on the assumption that some events are truly random, the first part of this axiom falls. The second part seems plainly contradictory, but since a great number of contemporary philosophers have persistently defended the rationality of holding that free will and determinism are compatible, it will patently require some ingenuity on my part to show the opposite.

The great difficulty in conceiving of God is that any language we use to speak of him appears on the surface to treat God as one object in the universe; admittedly, perhaps, one object in another storey of the universe than the storey consisting of all the material objects in space and time. But God, if he is indeed the creator of the material universe of space and time, cannot be one object in that universe or in an enlarged universe that consists of the material universe and heaven, and cannot be the universe as a whole, particularly if it can be shown that the visible universe began. Even if we speak to God in prayer as though he were another person like us in our universe, we have to acknowledge that he is not like that, but is beyond our material universe which exists in space and time. Yet that we can speak to him across that gap, and that he can speak to us is an irreducible part of at least Judaism and Christianity.

This relationship between God and human beings is not, however, unique. A scientist who considers a new theory proposed by another scientist is examining a theory proposed to him or to her as a statement of the case from a point of view outside the universe. If true, this new theory insofar as it asserts mathematical truths and relationships and uncertainties has always been true. The theory is not the personal possession of the scientist who proposed it. The scientist who

---

[2] Norman Kemp Smith (1935), p. 183; Wollheim (1963), p. 121.
[3] Norman Kemp Smith (1935), pp. 216, 247; Wollheim (1963), pp. 148, 175.

is now examining the new theory and trying to decide whether to give up the old theory and adopt the new is not trying to decide whether the theory suits a set of deep personal dispositions. If the theory overthrows the theory held by the second scientist who was elected to the Royal Society on the basis of that old theory, the second scientist must not allow the pain of abandoning the old theory to stand in the way of adopting the new theory, if the new theory turns out, in fact, to be true. The new theory stands in relation to the universe about which it is a theory in an analogous relation of God to the universe. Both scientists stand in a relationship to the new theory in an analogous way to the way the person praying stands to God to whom he or she prays.

"Not even in the case of our own life is the intellectual nature shut up within the boundary of the flesh ... the soul by the movements of its thinking faculty can coincide at will with the whole of creation. It ascends to the heavens, and sets foot within the deep ... in the restlessness of its curiosity..."[4]

Similarly, when a friend proposes to me that the action I am contemplating would be wrong or mean or cruel, that friend is asking me to assess my proposed action against a standard that exists to which my friend directs my attention. I may, of course, argue that the alleged meanness or cruelty is simply a partial assessment of my proposed action which, on a longer view, is generous and loving. But here, too, I am appealing to a standard that I can expect my friend to be able to see and accept. Bernard Williams, it is true, denies that the adoption of the point of view of the universe (to use Henry Sidgwick's terminology) is possible; "there is simply no conceivable exercise that consists in stepping completely outside myself and from that point of view evaluating *in toto* the dispositions, projects, and affections that constitute the substance of my own life."[5] This denial of the analogy of ethics with scientific theory leads Williams to the conclusion that "there is no coherent ethical theory."[6] However, he is claiming implicitly to espouse the ethical theory that there is no coherent ethical theory. He expects me to adopt his theory and, presumably, blames me for not accepting it as true, for he speaks much of the "demands

---

[4] Gregory of Nyssa, *Great Catechism*, chapter 10.
[5] "The point of view of the universe", The Henry Sidgwick Memorial Lecture, Newnham College, Cambridge, 7 May 1982 reprinted in Williams (1995), pp. 153-71 at p. 169.
[6] Williams (1995), p. 171.

of truthfulness" required in philosophy and by philosophy.[7] Yet he thinks blame is, in part, a fiction.[8] Since Williams argues "responsibility does not entail 'I could have acted otherwise'"[9] he is committed to arguing "rationality does not entail 'I could have thought otherwise'". But rationality requires us to belong to a community of thinkers that is prepared, in the face of a good argument, to say just this. Bernard Williams pretends to try to persuade anyone who holds that determinism and moral responsibility are incompatible that they are wrong. If he succeeded, that person would have to say, "I was wrong in holding a flawed argument to be true; I could have thought otherwise; I was responsible for a mistake." "Philosophical practice makes strenuous moral demands", writes Ronald Hepburn. Among those demands is "the strength of character to change one's mind on basic beliefs, and to follow the argument rather than one's emotional leanings."[10]

In other words, anyone who thinks about morality, or anyone who thinks, is committed to assessing those thoughts from a point of view outside of the thinker's own dispositions, projects and affections. This point of view is analogous to the point of view that Judaism and Christianity take to be the point of view of God in relation to the universe. Just as there is commerce across the gap between the thinker's own dispositions, projects and affections and the point of view of truth outside that universe, so there is commerce across the gap between the human being and God.

The second root of modern atheism is to be found in two related assumptions, the assumption that there is no such thing as chance and the assumption that determinism and free will are compatible.

Peter L. Bernstein in his book, *Against the Gods: The Remarkable Story of Risk* argues that "the revolutionary idea that defines the boundary between modern times and the past is the mastery of risk."[11] The turning point was when Blaise Pascal showed how to calculate the proportionate pay-out of the staked money when a game of chance was interrupted and could not be completed. In other words, he calculated the effect future chance events would have in relation to the entirely fixed events that had already transpired in the course of the game to that point. At the heart of the problem was the recogni-

---

[7] E.g. Williams (1996), p. 18.
[8] "How free does the will need to be", Williams (1995), pp. 3-21 at p. 16.
[9] Williams (1995), p. 17.
[10] Hepburn (1995), pp. 665-66 at p. 665.
[11] Bernstein (1996), p. 1.

tion that the odds of a perfectly spun perfect penny landing heads was exactly one in two.

Similarly, the theory of natural selection rests on the assumption that random mutations have occurred in the inert matter of the universe to produce living organisms, and that random mutations occur in the living organisms that turn out to be successful. Success breeds success.

We now know that chance is an absolutely essential characteristic of the world; we would not be here to discuss the question were it not for the occurrence of absolutely random events. At the heart of the universe lies what Frank Ramsey called a "principle of indifference."[12] Any attempt to explain any occurrence in this world relies on the observation that the event we label a cause is connected with the event we label an effect by the steady lack of randomness in the occurrence of the two events. Unless there were an indifference there could not be significant regularity.

But how do we know the principle of indifference? The widespread popular belief in scientific circles that this principle has been established by experiment is, of course, false. No series of experiments with tossing perfectly balanced coins an enormous number of times would establish the principle that the odds of heads is exactly one in two. Should we find 10 to the power of 1000 plus one heads against 10 to the power of 1000 tails, we would not doubt the principle of indifference. But nor would this experiment prove the principle. Of course we are confirmed in our belief in the principle by its very success, but the principle itself we simply have to accept as a principle governing the universe. We did not make it up; we have discovered it.

From this principle follows an important conclusion about time. If there is chance, then the future is not fixed. If time is to continue into the future, there are limitations on what can transpire; there are impossibilities. But if time is to continue and there are to be chance events, we do not know what those chance events will be. The past and the future are not symmetrical: in the past lie actual events, but for the future we are able to envisage possible events that may be realized, potential events. Not every potentiality will be realized, and many different potentialities are present now.[13]

---

[12] Ramsey (1931), p. 210.
[13] For the opposite argument, see Sprigge (1993), pp. 486-90 *et passim*.

The second part of this widespread modern view is that determinism and free will are compatible.

Before we turn to the compatibilist position, let us first be clear as to what makes determinism so attractive to the modern mind. The attractiveness lies in the ploy which exploits the desire of the defender of free will to preserve human responsibility. The determinist turns on the defender of free will and says, So you want to preserve space for human responsibility? You want to be able to say of actions that they are *my* actions. But "to call an action mine is to bring it into relation with my past actions and the personality that I and others know."[14] The objection is that I can only be truly responsible for how I decide to act if I am responsible for my principles of choice. But to be responsible for my principles of choice I must have chosen them by principles of choice; and these principles of choice by other principles, and so on in endless regress. Accordingly, neither I nor anyone else is ever responsible, because neither I nor anyone else has ever chosen freely. As Ayers puts this position—a position which he sets out to refute—"Why should a man be held responsible for something supposed to be unrelated to all antecedents and perhaps to all that comes afterwards, something that came into his head from nowhere?"[15]

The answer to this objection to determinism turns on the nature of a responsible act. A free act is not necessarily a responsible act. The point can best be shown by reminding ourselves of how a sheep dog is trained. At St Abb's Head my wife and I once met a shepherd driving sheep. He had a young eighteen-months-old sheep dog who, he said, was too ready simply to follow the old dog, not ready to strike out on his own. The shepherd said that he had both to give him the confidence to take initiatives and to keep him obedient. The freedom of our actions consists in choosing to actualize one of the potentialities that are open to us, potentialities governed by our circumstances, our previous decisions and our hereditary capabilities.[16] Full responsibility comes when we are able to justify our actions to ourselves or to others. A responsible act is an act taken either on the grounds that the act is the right thing to do in the circumstances or on the grounds that, if it is the wrong thing to do, I take responsibility for any consequences that will flow from it. Of course my decision to act is governed by the actual possibilities that are open to me both by

---

[14] Ayers (1968), p. 5, paraphrasing C.D. Broad.
[15] Ayers (1968), pp. 3-4.
[16] Ayers (1968), pp. 152, 154 *et passim*.

the circumstances and by my past decisions and capabilities. But when I say, I am responsible for this act that I am going to do, the thing that I am going to do is a responsible act not because it is entirely mine (though it is mine) but it becomes a responsible act because I hold that it is right. The true principle on which I act is not endlessly chosen by true principles but is chosen because it is true. There is no possible prior justification for its truth. If I choose to act immorally, of course, then I bring forward reasons and prior conditions in order to justify the immoral act, such as that I am obliged to act and the only courses of action open to me are immoral. But I never can justify acting morally by appealing to reasons in the previous circumstances of my life. It would be absurd to say that I am going to tell the truth because I have been brought up to tell the truth.

The determinist who mounts the argument about responsibility is right to insist that a defender of free will has to face the problem that a satisfactory answer to the problem of responsibility that avoids the deterministic description of responsibility has not been found.[17] But the determinist who makes this reasonable demand on any defender of free will is relying on the truth of a self-evident kind, that old unrefuted arguments have to be refuted if one wishes to overthrow them. The determinist is not appealing to a history of responsible decisions that have been taken in the past which issue in this responsible decision to lay on the defender of free will this requirement. The determinist is appealing to an argument that both the determinist and the defender of free will have to accept if they are to be responsible arguers. My argument is that the defender of determinism is assuming a view of responsibility that the argument being put forward by the determinist denies.

There has recently been advanced a sophisticated view of the compatibilism of free will and determinism that concedes the self-conscious assumption we all have that we are free but argues that the nature of our self-consciousness precludes us from ever being conscious of the fact that all things are determined.

The thesis was, I think, first proposed by Chomsky, but it has been most fully developed by Colin McGinn.[18] Things are determined in all respects but our consciousness is precluded by the nature of things from ever being able to be conscious of this, so that we must continue

---

[17] As for example, Galen Strawson, reviewing John Thorp, *Free Will: A Defence against Neurophysiological Determinism* (London: Routledge & Kegan Paul, 1980) in *TLS* 16 January 1981, p. 62.
[18] McGinn (1991).

to be conscious that we have freedom; "the only way to avoid being checkmated by consciousness is to assume you do not understand it", as he put it in the *Times Higher Education Supplement*, 5 April 1996.

That argument is not impregnable. The thesis itself is a thesis of which we are all conscious, and that means that we are either conscious that it is right or that it is wrong. But that example of consciousness (whether it be a consciousness that the thesis is true or a consciousness that the thesis is false) is (by virtue of the hypothesis) something that is in fact determined, even though we can never be conscious that it is determined. Accordingly our consciousness that the thesis is either true or false is a false consciousness, for consciousness entails the idea that we can make meaningful choices which (according to the thesis) is an illusion. But in that case we can be conscious that our consciousness is an illusion and the thesis fails. It is not even possible to think a contradiction, that an action is both free and not free; one proposition must yield to the other.[19]

However, McGinn has more recently stated a much stronger hypothesis. In a review of P.M.S. Hacker's *Wittgenstein's Place in Twentieth-Century Analytic Philosophy* in the *Times Literary Supplement* of 3 January 1997 he throws down, right at the end, a bold challenge to most contemporary philosophy. "My own suspicion is that there is really only one alternative left [to the only other possibility, the possibility of solving the traditional problems of philosophy by either mere conceptual investigation or by empirical science]: that the problems of philosophy are not solvable by any method of inquiry available to the human mind. The mistake is to think that we can do anything to solve, or resolve, our deepest philosophical perplexities, we can only articulate them ever more finely."

McGinn is not making the entirely unexceptional statement that there can be true propositions that are not known to be true. By posing the question, Are the problems of philosophy solvable by any method of inquiry available to the human mind? he is questioning the ability of the human mind to solve any of its problems. He is implying that mere conceptual investigation and empirical science have proved impotent. His question is, by any test, the deepest of our philosophical perplexities, for it concerns the basic ability of the human mind itself to solve problems, and it assumes the futility of the usual lines of approach. Unless we can be confident of the power of the human mind to solve problems, we can hardly argue; we cannot endure the

---

[19] C.A. Campbell (1957), p. 385.

thought that our attempts at argument are illusory, however open we are to the idea that our attempts at argument may well contain mistakes.

Let us suppose that the solution is No, the problems of philosophy are not solvable by any method of inquiry available to the human mind. Then we have solved one of the deepest philosophical perplexities and there is at least one exception to the rule. And this is not any old exception; it is a solution to the fundamental question about the reliability of our reasoning. The assumption that all our problem solving is illusory would cut at the root of all our other processes of reasoning. However, we do not have to worry, because such an answer would contradict itself; it would solve the Queen of problems and would accordingly disprove the thesis it is pretending to maintain.

Let us suppose that the solution is Yes, the problems of philosophy are solvable by some method of inquiry available to the human mind. Then we have not solved the perplexity but merely set ourselves an endless task. We can never be confident that, having convinced ourselves that we have solved the half-dozen or so main problems of philosophy (such as the mind-body problem, the problem of time, the problem of causation), *either* that we have solved them *or* that they are all the problems that have to be solved.

So McGinn has directed our attention to a most interesting feature of problem solving. The very fact that we can pose the problem, Are the problems of philosophy solvable by any method of inquiry available to the human mind? *either* involves us in a contradiction (if we answer No) *or* involves us in a quest to which there is no end (however successful or not we may be from time to time), the quest to solve problem after problem that is posed to us by the way things are. We must answer, Yes, the problems of philosophy are solvable by some method of inquiry available to the human mind, but we cannot be sure that the answer is Yes, for the only way we can proceed is to try to solve all the problems we know about, and to keep our eyes open for some problems that we have not yet clearly discerned. We have to believe that the problems are in principle solvable by methods of inquiry available to the human mind, but we can never finally prove that they are.

It follows that the conclusion that we cannot coherently prove that the answer is No, there are problems of philosophy not solvable by any methods of inquiry known to the human mind (because we would then have produced an answer to the deepest of those problems), involves us in accepting at least one axiom that is given without being able to be proved, the axiom that all other problems of philosophy are solvable by the methods of inquiry open to the human mind. Furthermore, because no procedure available to the human mind can get final certainty that we have actually solved these problems, nor final certainty that we have in fact discovered all the problems, we are forced all the time to live by faith in the axiom just mentioned.

That leads us towards a very interesting indication that God exists. There is no doubt that the human mind can pose the problem, Are there problems of philosophy that are not solvable by any method of inquiry known to the human mind? Behind that question is the tacit assumption that there must be a mind, even if not a human mind, that can solve the problem, because the very existence of something we can label as a problem assumes that there is a power that guarantees that problems can be set, and therefore a power that guarantees that sometimes, at least, there are solutions. Computers do not have problems nor do they pose problems, only sets of conditions which they are programmed to deal with and sets of results that I know raise problems but they don't; my computer does not know that I am dealing with a problem posed by McGinn, even though it is very efficiently producing lines of type on the problem that raise problems for you, the listener, if not for me, the author. However, we all know problems that we cannot at the moment solve, but we have to hang on to the assumption that either there is a solution, or that we have mistaken sheer chaos for a problem.

All problem-solving human beings therefore live by an axiom that is given but that cannot be proved, the confidence that all the other problems bar this one are solvable by the methods of inquiry open to the human mind. What is given implies a giver, whom we are accustomed to call God. All our problem solving depends on Him.

Can we avoid the conclusion that God exists?

Nietzsche saw this problem clearly. "Ich fürchte, wir werden Gott nicht los, weil wir noch an die Grammatik glauben..."; "I fear we are not getting rid of God because we still believe in grammar..."[20] The order and rationality of our grammar, and of all our attempts to make sense of the universe render it difficult to jettison belief in God.

---

[20] *Götzen-Dämmerung oder Wie man mit dem Hammer philosophiert* III "Die 'Vernunft' in der Philosophie" §5, end; *Twilight of the Idols and The Anti-Christ* (tr. R.J.Hollingdale; Harmondsworth: Penguin, 1968), p. 38.

Can we explain explaining? It is relatively easy to explain mistakes. We may have to hunt for the reason, but once we are pretty sure a conclusion is false, we can usually find out why, if we take the trouble. We look for faulty processes in the work of those who made the mistakes, for accidental faults in the apparatus used, for limitations in the scope of the observations or reasoning.

It is much more difficult to show that a conclusion is true. Of course we eliminate the alleged mistakes pointed out by those who oppose our conclusions, but we can never cover all possible mistakes and, in any case, the mistakes we still have made may not matter.

The only way, in the end, that we can show that a conclusion is true is to show that it is true. We point.

The curious thing is that we never try to prove the reliableness and the connectedness of the universe. When we discuss whether or not a particular hypothesis is true, we are assuming that it is an example of the reliableness and the connectedness of things in the universe. That, we have simply to assume. The universe which we did not make ourselves is reliably open to the calculation of objective probabilities and to the objective explanation of all the processes in it.

If the question of the existence of God is not capable of rational decision, nor can the question of the rationality of the universe be rationally decided, for it can never be the subject of rational enquiry. Yet we have to assume it in order to think. Could it not be that the existence of God is the same?

At 4 p.m. on Friday 22 February 1991 Philosophy and Divinity met together in the Martin Hall, New College, The Mound, Edinburgh to hear a paper on "Religious Imagination" from Professor Ronald Hepburn. Professor James Mackey was in the chair. At the end of the paper, Professor Mackey made a substantial contribution, and then began a more general discussion. Both George and Elspeth Davie were present. Elspeth Davie is best known for her short stories and novels, but she is a philosopher trained. She said, "Do you believe in God? You can't say Yes or No. Very few questions are like that. Whether you believe in God, it's not clear cut." She was latching on to Professor Hepburn's argument about the tension between the religious imagination, which seems to be leading us on to some sort of belief in God, and critical argument, which seems to scupper all attempts to find a metaphysical justification for such belief. On another occasion he spoke of the possibility "that the aesthetic experience may keep alive some view of the world that the concepts of systematic metaphysical thought cannot precisely articulate, nor its arguments support. (The fact that we have no satisfactory account of the relation between body and mind may mean that we lack the necessary concepts to make it intelligible; but certainly does not compel us to deny our experience of both!)"[21]

I wish to suggest that belief in the existence of God is inescapable, but that there are good reasons why the question still remains open in the way Elspeth Davie so vividly put it: "You can't say Yes or No."

Do you concede that we may pose the question, Does God Exist? Then, if God does not exist, either of two possibilities must follow, and no other.

The first possibility is that the persistence of things and thoughts and their orderly change inheres in their own natures and the interaction between them. Then it follows that our posing of the question and our expectation that our answers will be true or false is an illusion because whatever happens had to be what would happen, and there can be no false answers and therefore no true answers either. In a determined system any true answers are only accidentally true, so far as we are concerned. We are all actors in a play written by fate for which there is no audience. We never stop acting in the play. If, in playing our parts, we say something true, and some of our fellow actors tell us that what we have said is true, that is only the part we and they play, and there is no audience to judge whether what we actors say is true is true or false. The determinist's assumption that there is an audience is another illusion, like the illusion that what is judged (in the play) a true answer is actually true.

The second possibility is that we can never be sure that our question will stay the same whether written down or remembered, nor that the conclusions drawn from evidence adduced for or against our hypotheses will hold even while we are considering the question. Then it follows that our questioning is futile.

But you concede that the question, Does God exist?, may be posed and that a true answer is possible. Therefore God exists.[22]

You may object to this argument that a third possibility could follow, if God did not exist, namely, that the universe consists of a combination of events that are governed by iron laws and of events that are chance.

I reply that either the combination of fixed events and chance events is fixed by iron laws or the combination of fixed events and

---

[21] Hepburn (1996), pp. 200-201.
[22] O'Neill (1980), p. 15.

chance events is random. If the combination of fixed events and random events is fixed by iron laws, there can be no false answers and therefore no true answers either. If the combination of fixed events and random events is fixed by chance, then we can never be sure whether our provisional answers to any question are fixed or random, and our questioning is equally futile.

Since you concede that the question, Does God exist? may be posed and that a true answer is possible, and since it seems that no other possible state of affairs exists that enables us to pose this question and discuss it, then God exists.

In other words, the assumed reliability of our thinking seems to require the existence of a power that guarantees to us that reliability, even should we use that power to deny His existence.

A powerful reason for the seemingly eternal possibility of saying, No to the existence of God perhaps lies in Gödel's Theorem. Gödel argued that, "if arithmetic is consistent, its consistency cannot be established by any meta-mathematical reasoning that can be represented within the formalism of arithmetic."[23] If we may extend this principle, it becomes, If our thought is consistent—and that is what we all aim at—then its consistency cannot be established by any metaphysical reasoning that can be represented within the formalism of our reasoning. Once we grasp this conclusion of the Liar Paradox, it is seductively easy to turn stoic and to plead humble. We can glory in the essential provisionalness of human reasoning and conclude that, if we human beings cannot explain everything, then we'll be damned if we allow that there is a God who can.

But the main case for adopting provisionally the answer, No, is summed up in Hamm's remark in Samuel Beckett's *Endgame*, "The bastard! He doesn't exist!"

Hamm:	Let us pray to God.
Clov:	Again!
Nagg:	Me sugar-plum!
Hamm:	God first! (*Pause.*) Are you right?
Clov:	(*resigned*). Off we go.
Hamm:	(*to Nagg*). And you?
Nagg:	(*clasping his hands, closing his eyes, in a gabble*). Our Father which art—

---

[23] This is the summary given by Nagel and Newman (1959; paperback ed., 1971), p. 96.

Hamm:	Silence! In silence! Where are your manners? (*Pause.*) Off we go. (*Attitudes of prayer. Silence. Abandoning his attitude, discouraged.*) Well?
Clov:	(*abandoning his attitude*). What a hope! And you?
Hamm:	Sweet damn all! (*To Nagg.*) And you?
Nagg:	Wait! (*Pause. Abandoning his attitude.*) Nothing doing!
Hamm:	The bastard! He doesn't exist!
Clov:	Not yet.
Nagg:	Me sugar-plum!
Hamm:	There are no more sugar-plums![24]

Could the Problem of Evil be part of the case for believing in God?

The problem of evil is that God, who is supposed to be all-powerful and all-loving, permits suffering which he would have blamed us for not preventing if we were present and had the power to avert it. By the morality he is supposed to have imposed on us he himself is condemned.

Let us start from a fact that I think the atheist would concede, that even if God did not exist, there would remain a certain type of problem of evil. I make this evil, normally labelled a problem, the basis of an argument from evil to the existence of God.

There is a common human awareness that fate is hard, that virtue is not only not rewarded but sometimes seemingly punished. This common human awareness contains within it an extraordinarily far-reaching assumption. We all seem to assume, whether or not we believe in God, that virtue should be rewarded and vice should be punished. We gasp in horror at the end of Oliver Twist when Bill Sykes slips and the rope hangs him, but we also know he got no less than he deserved. The novelist Judith O'Neill and her agent discussed the fate of the Australian woman schoolteacher in *Deepwater*, who, during the Great War, stirred up the children she taught and their parents to persecute the German descendants who were their neighbours. The problem they discussed was whether she comes to a sticky enough end in having to live as wife to a bad-tempered soldier who was blinded at Gallipoli. They were discussing an objective problem.

Whether or not we believe in God, we all know what it is to sue for mercy. Suing for mercy entails I know that I deserve punishment, I know the punishment is more than I can bear, and I could recognize

---

[24] Beckett (1958), pp. 37-38.

some penance imposed by the one I had harmed (or an impartial observer) as penance indeed and not punishment.

The problem of evil arises for those who do not believe in God and for those who do, because everyone knows there is an objective relationship between good deeds and reward, and evil deeds and punishment. Of course, this relationship is not easy to establish, and almost any set of events in which human beings have acted may become, for the sensitive observer, an almost insoluble problem of moral discrimination. Yet, however difficult the issue may be, it remains a problem calling for moral discrimination; that is, we assume there is an exact relationship between the action of the moral agent, the praise or blame attaching to that action, and the reward or punishment due. It may be hard to decide whether a particular act of divorce was right or wrong, but we assume it was at one end of the scale or the other. Similarly, and this is the nub of my argument, we assume the subsequent happiness of the genuinely innocent partner deserved and the subsequent happiness of the guilty partner a problem.

We assume from the "general course of things" that by exerting ourselves we obtain some degree of enjoyment and that by "rashness, ungoverned passion, wilfulness, or even negligence" we may make ourselves miserable.[25] From that regularity, which has many painful exceptions, in the happiness of the wicked and the misery of the just, we jump to a rule.

These assumptions are, of course, unprovable, in the sense that there is no book I can consult or no court I can go to on earth that will tell me whether my assumption and yours was right. Yet we all assume we are right to discuss praise and blame, and right to measure praise and blame against reward and punishment. Anyone who seeks to eliminate praise and blame from our language cannot help praising those who most nearly succeed, and blaming those who fail; and the praise and blame are, for those who admire and attack the philosopher who mounts this campaign, reward and punishment.

We all concede that the reward of evil and the punishment of good is a problem, and no series of disasters, even disasters on the scale of Auschwitz, will upset our rule and make flagrant evil cease to be a problem. The law that evil deserves punishment and good deserves reward is simply what we know to be true. It is the law by which we measure all that happens to us, and all that happens to all people everywhere.

---

[25] Butler, *Analogy* I, chapter II.

The law we did not invent, nor did our ancestors. As soon as Eve knew she was *homo sapiens* she knew this law. Adam also became *sapiens* when he saw what he was capable of doing to Eve. They also soon came to know that the laws they taught their children were just and unjust according as they conformed or failed to conform to the law of justice they discovered to be in place already. They helped their children to a quicker apprehension of the law they would have discovered anyway by rewarding and punishing them gently according to the standard of reward and punishment they knew existed before they were conscious of it.

Eventually, with God's help (I would argue), some thinkers came to see clearly what was the case, that this law about the proper apportioning of praise and blame was given by the one true God. Just as all thinking people can see that you always have to justify telling a lie, so all thinking people can see that virtue should always be rewarded and vice punished, without needing to believe in the one true God. Nevertheless, more persistent thought, aided by the help of divine grace which is (I believe) always available to the thinker, will lead to the conclusion that this law of reward and punishment is ordained by the one true God.

I have not tried to mitigate in the least the problem of evil. My case is that the stubborn persistence of the problem, even for the atheist, is an argument for the existence of God.

2

Barth on the Heart of the Matter

The bankrupt atheism of modern thought has deeply penetrated Christian theology. Serious thinking people who want to see the point of it all need not only to be warned of the fallacies lying behind much modern thought but also to be warned that the same fallacies may be found in the work of theologians to whom they might wish to turn for help in worshipping God. I have deliberately chosen one theologian, Karl Barth (1886–1968), who is widely credited with having "faced more directly than any other Christian thinker of our time the menace to Christian belief presented by Humanism. To a Humanism which understands itself, the ideas of God, sin and death have lost all importance, except as symbols which proved of temporary advantage in the past. Barth replies that there is a living God, and that God has spoken."[1]

Historical criticism and the heart of the matter

Barth rightly saw that historical criticism had done much to shake confidence in the reliability of the Bible and therefore confidence in the reliability of what the Bible taught about God. *Die Sache*, the heart of the matter, he said, "is the relation between God and man."[2]

> "God is in heaven and you are on earth." The relation of *this* God to *this* man, the relation of *this* man to *this* God is for me the theme of the Bible and the sum of philosophy in one. The philosophers call this crisis of human knowing "the origin, the first principle." The Bible sees at this crossroad Jesus Christ.

Barth's sole concern was to keep as steadily as possible in view what the nineteenth-century Danish theologian Kierkegaard called "the

---

[1] Mackintosh (1937), p. 317.
[2] Barth (1923), answer to Harnack's first thesis.

infinite qualitative difference" between time and eternity.³ His constant theme is revelation, "transcendent revelation" which "comes from outside man and the cosmos."⁴

Barth argued that historical criticism of the Bible, in relation to the heart of the matter, is a matter of relative indifference. Historical criticism can, it is true, perform a preparatory function in establishing what stands there in the text by means of translation and paraphrase of the words of the text.⁵ Historical criticism can, perhaps, do more: it can establish that the content of the gospel can be communicated, according to the gospel itself, only by the action of the content itself. God's revelation only occurs when God reveals himself to human beings. In other words, historical knowledge of the gospel shows that by historical knowledge one cannot know the gospel. The same holds for critical reflection.⁶

Barth sides with Lessing in Lessing's plea to Lutheran theologians of his day to have done with all attempts historically to ground or to justify or to defend revelation as an historical entity: "Revelation has to be understood at all costs as a fact grounded in itself, that is as a fact neither historically vulnerable nor historically provable, but in itself certain."⁷ Lessing wanted to get over the "broad ugly ditch" from historical truths to a completely different class of truths by discerning a revelation in history, the whole course of history, but Barth will not follow him there, for Lessing denies what Barth calls "special, indeed, uniquely qualified historical truth [which] descends from above [and] confronts all other historical truth from without." On Lessing's terms, there is no Lord of history *within* history, nor can there be a Lord of history who is also *over* history.⁸

Barth does not simply hold that historical grounds cannot be urged in support or proof of revelation; he positively relishes the problematic nature of the truths historians discover. "The more clearly the biblical witnesses of Jesus Christ speak, the more what they say gets lost in what we should today call the realm of pure legend."⁹ It was Karl Barth who said about Christ's tomb, "This grave might be proved to be finally closed or open; it is really all the same. What use

---

³ Barth (1922), Vorwort zur zweiten Auflage, xiii; English, p. 10.
⁴ Barth (1948b), p. 208.
⁵ Barth (1922), Vorwort, x; English, p. 6; (1923), answer to Harnack's third thesis.
⁶ Barth (1923), answer to Harnack's first thesis.
⁷ Barth (1947), p. 222; English, pp. 133-34.
⁸ Barth (1947), pp. 234-35; English, pp. 146-48.
⁹ Barth (1948b), p. 222.

is the grave proved closed or open near Jerusalem in the year 30?"[10] He avoided this sort of remark in later years, but there is no reason to think that he changed his mind. In 1955 he could still write:

> The assertion "Christ is risen" admittedly implies the assertion, "A dead man has come to life again" together with the assertion of his grave's having been found *empty*. But it only *implies* it. If this second assertion were abstracted from the first, it would consequently—whether affirmed or either denied or demythologized—become *entirely without interest* for the understanding of the text and its witness.[11]

Barth does not care whether or not anyone says that Jesus' body was raised to life and transformed; he is aware that the term "resurrection" means just that, for it was the issue that divided contemporary Pharisees and Sadducees from one another; and he is aware that H.J. Holtzmann and Albert Schweitzer argued that only an empty tomb could have prompted the proclamation of the resurrection, although these two great scholars believed that the body had been moved, not that a miracle had been brought about by God. Barth does not care what people want to say on the issue, so long as they do not say that the resurrection was a miracle, an actual new happening in the course of ordinary history, for that would be to abstract it from Barth's own particular way of talking about God and Christ.

It was Barth who said, years before Rudolf Bultmann wrote his book on Jesus, "Whoever still does not understand that we Christians know Christ no longer after the flesh, should have it said by critical biblical scholarship: the more radically shocked he is, the better for him and for the matter (*die Sache*). And that could well be the service historical knowledge can perform for the true task of theology."[12]

At this point Barth really annoyed Bultmann. Bultmann was an exegete who thought accurate exegesis mattered.[13] Bultmann was also an historian, and believed he could on historical as well as philosophical grounds rule out certain claims made in the Gospels that miraculous events had occurred. Bultmann suspected Barth agreed, but Barth refused to be drawn. Why? Barth relied more on Lessing's argument that reports of past events were too uncertain to base anything on, than on Lessing's philosophical belief that miracles could not in principle

---

[10] Barth (1925), 2nd. ed., p. 78.
[11] Barth (1955), KD IV/2, p. 166; CD IV/2, p. 149.
[12] Barth (1923), answer to Harnack's 14th thesis.
[13] Bultmann to Barth, commenting on some of Barth's exegetical judgments in four issues of the periodical *Theologische Existenz*, Marburg, 10.xii.1935; see Barth (1971), p. 162; 2nd ed., pp. 160-61.

happen. Barth really thought historical and exegetical investigation was unimportant beside the heart of the matter. He laughed at the seriousness of the exegetes, and to demonstrate his high good humour about exegesis, he indulged in exegesis with the greatest pleasure, not caring a damn about what the professionals thought. He believed that he was preserved from serious error by his unremitting concentration on *die Sache*, the thing itself. That could not be discovered through any other minor discoveries, for that discovery was nothing more than the discovery itself: God, revealer revealed and revealedness.

Historical investigation is a trifling matter beside the great matters of revelation: like a tiny alpine hut in a deep valley between two four thousand metre mountains.

> Christ who died for our sins, Christ raised on the third day, Christ End and Beginning is not to be proved [by investigating the grave], and yet he is manifest, whom the παράδοσις [the tradition of the early church and Paul following the tradition] decidedly sets forth ἐν πρώτοις, as the *Hauptsache* [the main thing]. But the grave, the thing that could be proved, stands in the middle [of these two other assertions] as an alpine hut in the deep valley between two four-thousand-metre mountains put there almost with a certain irony, one could say (if the matter wasn't so absolutely serious) as a contrast to what here to left and right is being witnessed to—without being able to be proved, nay, as proving itself; and that is how it is to be believed.[14]

How was Barth so sure that ἐτάφη (he was buried) in 1 Cor 15 was a little alpine hut? There are exegetical arguments, and Barth deployed them: the other two on each side have "according to the scriptures" attached, and this does not. But his main argument is that the nature of the matter in hand demands this conclusion. His argument in the foreword to the second edition of *Romans* was that if he paid concentrated attention to this "matter", he would be bound to produce a faithful reading of the text.

> The exposition alone can decide whether and how far I have succeeded in carrying through my assumption. If it is false; if Paul was really talking about something other than the permanent crisis of time and eternity, why, then I should find myself led *ad absurdum* in the course of his text itself. Should anyone indeed ask me further on what grounds I approached Romans according to this assumption, I would answer with the counter-question, whether any serious man could possibly approach a text that was

---

[14] Barth (1925), 2nd. ed., p. 78.

not unworthy of serious attention except according to the assumption that—God is God?[15]

The upshot is that, if you recognize the existence of critical historical questions, you should follow Barth and laugh at them—these things are put there to tease us—; if you don't, you should be an old-fashioned believer who simply accepts the Bible as given and self-authenticating. The two camps to be avoided like the plague are D.F. Strauss–Athur Drews–Rudolf Bultmann, who consign the historical kernel to such obscurity that it could be all myth, on the one side; and the "positive theologians," who try to see in the documents historical events just like other historical events, on the other side.

> In history in itself there is nothing, so far as the eye can see, that was able to found belief ... In history as such everything could always have been also taken in quite another way. Stick unequivocally to the [insight] that faith is founded on *revelation*, on *historical* revelation, but on revelation; and accustom oneself to think of revelation as a special category and an inseparable unity of event, speech and hearing—[for that is] how it is actually witnessed to in the Bible. Whoever will find revelation, he must find *it* and not something else, not merely that which revelation *also* is [i.e. history?]. Otherwise he finds revelation not at all.[16]

Bultmann moved from the alleged necessity that one could not even conceive of finding evidence of God's working in the world to the realm of "*my* world," where natural necessity becomes the existential recognition of limitation, godlessness, and despair. Bultmann pointed out that both these moves were moves made by some philosophers who both believed that all natural events originated and operated according to laws and who saw that men were put in a predicament by this state of affairs of knowing they should be free without being able to see how they could be free.

Bultmann was stuck with his structurally faulted system which asserted *both* that man had to be delivered by an event from outside *and* that there could not be an outside from with anything could come.[17]

Barth, one suspects, could not see a way round Bultmann's first step, but in any case he is in principle unable to argue with Bultmann, for that would be to do natural theology. He simply asserts—which is true—that men do use electric light and listen to the radio while still entertaining the idea that there are other more pressing concerns, that

---

[15] Barth (1922), Introduction p. xiv; cf. English, pp. 10-11.
[16] Barth (1927), p. 237.
[17] Ogden (1961), "The structural inconsistency of Bultmann's solution", pp. 130-47.

they are not forbidden also to recognize another truth. They can freely believe in Jesus Christ risen from the dead without being committed to an implicit faith in a world of spirits and miracles. Barth asserts, and he laughs. He brands Bultmann's idea as a manifestation of the absurdly humourless Marburg tradition; people are not going to submit to dictatorship by the Marburg Kant school.[18]

Barth is right about Bultmann's system. His first move, the thesis about the closed law-bound world, and his second move, the thesis of the existentialists that humanity is caught in a trap, can only lead to a monologue between God and humanity, humanity and God. Barth asserts that:

> Jesus and his disciples in the Easter event are not a onesome but a twosome (*nicht einerlei sondern zweierlei*). He himself was with them in time, *beyond* the time which had unrolled from his birth to his death; now he was also with them in this time of revelation. That is what happened there [in the forty days].[19]

Barth's system, his great monument of lectures, papers, sermons, letters, pamphlets, books, and the *magnum opus*, his ten volumes of *Church Dogmatics*, is a holding operation. He knows that if he once let go of the permanent crisis between time and eternity, the question of the relation between God and humanity, the whole church and the whole of western civilization would collapse. He has to do what Mozart did, who lived in the shadow of the tremendous crisis in belief in God caused by the Lisbon earthquake of 1755, simply go on composing. As Barth said of Mozart, and could have said of himself,

> the problem of theodicy ... of critical or speculative reason ... lay unopposed behind him. Why should he worry about that? He had simply heard [one thing]—and he lets those who have ears to hear hear, up to this day simply hear this, which we at the end of the day will at once see: Providence in context (*die Schickung in Zusammenhang*) [Strophe 4 of the hymn by Christian Fürchtegott Gellert (1715-69), "Nach einer Prüfung kurzer Tage erwartet uns die Ewigkeit"]... Mozart makes audible the fact that creation praises its master *even* on the side that is turned towards nothingness, and so in its totality; and so creation is perfect.[20]

The trouble is that theology is not a symphony, however beautifully it is written. We must admit that Barth is one of the great masters of German prose, but we still have to ask the old questions, Is what he

---

[18] Barth (1948a), KD III/2, p. 536; CD III/2, p. 447.
[19] Barth (1948a), KD III/2, p. 534; CD III/2, p. 445..
[20] Barth (1950), KD III/3, pp. 337-39; CD III/3, pp. 297-99.

says true, is it consistent, is it coherent, is it morally admirable, is it clear what he is asserting and what denying?

He refuses his critics permission to ask these questions and if playing a church theologian were the same as playing in Drury Lane, he would be right.

Yet he has put his finger on a dilemma. The permanent crisis between time and eternity is the perennial problem of philosophy at least since Kant. Hegel saw that; and thought if only one kept one's eye on *die Sache*, the thing in itself, and lived through the movement of thought from *Wissen* to *Wesen* and from *Wesen* to *Ansichselbstsein*, from knowledge to what is there, and from what is there to what is for oneself, the whole could be preserved.[21] Barth wanted to keep God as the starting point and the ending point, not just *Geist* [Spirit]; but all he could say, like Hegel, was, Come with me on the journey and see if it doesn't all come clear and certain to you, too.

Unfortunately the therapy cannot work. All depends on the assertion that God is pure revelation. We are directed to a place where the revelation occurs, a place in history which is asserted to be the place of revelation by the Bible, but we are forbidden to ask what the revelation is of; we are forbidden to ask about God's existence, being, nature, law. We are told he loves humanity, but we are not told what he loves or why he loves, only that he also rejects humanity, as well; and that, fortunately for us, God's acceptance triumphs over his rejection, gospel over law. God is revelation: God the revealer, God the revealed, and God as revealedness, and there is nothing else to be said.

> For the Christian the revelation is itself the proof, the proof furnished by God himself. The Christian answer to the question of who and what God is, is a simple one: He is the subject who acts in His revelation. This act of revelation is a token of his Being and the expression of his nature.[22]

But to believe in such a God must be to believe without reasons, and belief like that is irrational. We abandon the reason and freedom we are bound to defend, if we are to talk sensibly to each other and to reflect on the world we see.

Barth has stubbornly defended revelation, at the cost of throwing away any defence.

To understand what Barth was getting at we have to remember that he was very much a member of a generation, a generation that received its formation in the years before World War I and then had to

---

[21] Hegel (1807), 1952 ed., p. 71.
[22] Barth (1948b), pp. 208-209.

try to cope with the disillusion and cynicism produced by the futility of the suffering during the war itself. This was a generation that saw through every pretension yet believed that by relentless and unremitting cynicism they could discover the secret of the whole universe that would bring utopia. They were philosophically sophisticated and well-schooled, these expressionists, but they despised the university schools of philosophy. Their characteristic mode of discourse was not argument but prophecy. "The cry drowned the word."[23] They thought that they were on the edge of a new way of understanding, a break-through of the eternal. The philosophy behind this was a flourishing idealism: the Kantians held annual conferences, and the followers of Schopenhauer met in the boardroom of the Deutsche Bank.[24] The dominant interpretation of Kant was that he preached we must behave *as if* God existed, *as if* the natural laws held, *as if* we had freedom, and *as if* we were eternal beings. The generation that saw through everything was yet able to affirm everything and to find paradise again. Ernst Bloch wrote that "... not only things but in the end even God is still the bushel over the light [Matt 5.15]; so the longing soul has to penetrate behind God himself." He ended his book on the *Spirit of Utopia* with these quasi-religious words.

> For only the wicked exist because of their God, but as for the righteous—there, God exists because of them, and in their hands is the hallowing of the name; the very naming of God is given to them: God who stirs in us and moves us, as dimly-discerned portal, darkest question, exalted inwardness; in the hands of philosophy devoted to God, in the hands of truth as prayer.[25]

Barth, of course, could not talk of getting behind God, but he certainly did talk of getting behind every other way of naming God besides his own. He explicitly compared his own non-systematic system to Kant's, and lined himself up with Kant as popularly interpreted in his day.[26] And Barth's only way of naming God was to will hollowness, the void, negation, where others had named God: "Faith is the will to the void, the deliberate perseverance in negation."[27]

His key doctrine was the doctrine of predestination.

---

[23] Ludwig Marcuse (1960), p. 70.
[24] Marcuse (1960), p. 63.
[25] Bloch (1923), pp. 305 and 365. Professor Wilfried Barner of Tübingen first drew my attention to the affinity of Barth's *Romans* with Ernst Bloch's *Geist der Utopie*.
[26] Barth (1920), p. 16.
[27] Barth (1923), p. 17; cf. English, p. 42.

> The doctrine of predestination is the sum of the gospel ... It is grounded in the confession [by us] of Jesus Christ because he is the predestinating God and predestinated humanity in one. The doctrine of predestination belongs accordingly to the doctrine of God because God, in that he elects humanity, not only decides on humanity, but also in a primordial sense decides on himself. The doctrine of predestination consists of the fundamental testimony to the eternal, free and everlasting grace as the beginning of all the ways and works of God.[28]

There is no purchase on God outside of this drama of predestination; Barth's sole message was to get us all to see that we were predestined. That was how we are to be drawn into being participants in the movement in which God not only decided to choose us, but even decided to choose himself. Once we are caught up into this drama, we see only Jesus Christ. He stands not only for the God who chooses us, but also for us who are chosen. In the end, Barth calls us to allow ourselves to be chosen by the God who, in choosing us, defines himself. Everything God does, he does to define us as his chosen ones. If God were a problem for us, he would not be God; "were we lacking clarity and certainty about God, were his existence a problem for us in the way the existence of other entities can be a problem for us, then it would definitely not be he who stood before us."[29]

There is no room for doubt, or for questioning. Surrender to God is everything. God cannot be argued with, as Job argued with him. God cannot be asked for anything, for everything we have and everything we do is now seen as the predestined destiny of us as part of all humanity. We cannot get any specific gifts from God. God cannot have mercy on one and not have mercy on another, for he has rejected everyone and chosen everyone—and election triumphs.[30] The ending of one of the prayers he offered in the Basel prison where, to his credit, he regularly took services, sums up his message. "Lord, simply because we believe and know that you have overcome and that, with you, we too have already overcome, we cry out to you: Show us nevertheless only the first steps of the embattled way of freedom! Amen."[31] Note the image of a journey, and note also that God's victory is also ours, without question. The prayer is nominally addressed to God, but really to the worshipper to get the worshipper to join Barth in the drama of his own theology.

---

[28] Barth (1942), KD II/2, § 32, heading, p. 1; cf. English, p. 3.
[29] Barth (1940), KD II/1, § 25, p. 42; cf. CD II/1, p. 39.
[30] Barth (1942), KD II/2, § 39.2, pp. 840-41; CD II/s, pp. 751-52.
[31] Barth (1963), p. 89.

Barth is the best humoured of theologians. Nothing can distress him. But he buys this serenity at the cost of making God a complete cypher from whom nothing can be asked or expected, except the endorsement of the fate of chosen humanity.

Barth, like Bultmann, accepted Lessing's "broad ugly ditch": on the one side the accidental truths of history; on the other side the necessary truths of reason. Barth tried to make his statements about God necessary, analytic, self-authenticating. It cannot be done. Even the most refined statement of necessary truth has to be examined to see if it is true. Accidental truths of history are always involved in establishing truth. For example, take the following two statements:

1. Today is either Saturday or not Saturday.
2. Today is both Saturday and not Saturday.

Both these statements are true, under certain circumstances: either this side of the international dateline, or both sides of the international date line.

What we singly and together hold to be true is a very complicated structure in which every part is connected with every other, however remotely. Our momentary observations, our settled convictions about what happened, our more general knowledge of what is the case, our theories about the world, our central beliefs are all subject to test and change for all sorts of reasons. But because everything is connected to everything else and because we are not alone, our systems are quite solid and stable. Our question is always, Is what we hold true or not? Naturally, not all systems are compatible, and there are many points at which they conflict. But for Barth there was only *one* conflict, over revelation, and there was no way of deciding the conflict except to decide it.

For example, Barth saw that Hitler was evil and opposed him. God be praised. But he did it for one reason: Hitler claimed to be as God. A true reason, but why should that assertion of revelation not be true? We had reasons, and we needed reasons for opposing Hitler. The same is true for belief in God: we have reasons and we need reasons.

Historical criticism is part of the system in which also exist statements about the relation of God to the world. The two sorts of statements must be connected. We have to be able to explore the connection, or else our statements about God and the world are empty.

3

What Would the Messiah Be Like?

The very question with which we begin, What would the Messiah be like?, has long been regarded as improper. Do we not know that there were hosts of anointed ones spoken of in the century or so before the destruction of Jerusalem and of the Second Temple? Do we not know that many Jewish writings make no reference to one figure who would be the decisive bringer in of the Kingdom of God? Do we not know that those writings that did mention a redeemer had contradictory visions of how that redemption would be achieved, who would be the main actors, whether it would result in a purely earthly paradise or a purely spiritual paradise, with all sorts of variations in between? Do we not know that, besides the Son of David, there were many other sorts of redeemer such as the Son of Man, the Anointed of Aaron, the Anointed of Joseph, the Prophet, the Teacher, the Prince of the Congregation, not to mention the two Anointed Ones, the Messiahs of Aaron and Israel? The most influential exponents of this view were George Foot Moore in 1920 and Morton Smith in 1959.

Morton Smith's article was called, "What is implied by the variety of messianic figures?" His thesis was simple. There are messiahs without Ends, that is, there were lots of people who were anointed by God, that anointing having nothing to do with the possible end of history. Also there are Ends without messiahs, that is, an enormous variety of pictures of what the End would be like in which only God and the angels were actors, with no particular redeemer. The Ends could vary from the establishment of ordinary kingdoms in this world, various forms of this world variously made over and improved, worlds entirely new and different, and spiritual bliss without any world at all. Quite contradictory theories could be preserved in the one document such as the *Ethiopic Book of Enoch* or the *Testaments of the Twelve Patriarchs*.

From this thesis Morton Smith drew a momentous conclusion. The fact that contradictory eschatologies were preserved by men who must have realized the discrepancies, and who obviously thought these eschatologies important by the care with which they preserved them, shows that eschatology could not have been the organizing principle of any Jewish communities of believers. There is no trace of "some unknown higher synthesis by which these many and apparently contradictory opinions were reconciled in a single system" and we have occasional evidence of polemic within single groups. Here are Morton Smith's crucial sentences:

> If a group had no single eschatological myth, it cannot have been organized as a community of believers in the myth it did not have. Nor can its cult acts be seen as dramatic representations or realizations of events which there was no single myth, accepted by all the members, to predict. If the variety of eschatological prediction is any evidence, eschatology was, for the members of these groups, a comparatively arbitrary and individual matter—part, and an important part, of their general *Weltanschauung*, but a part about which the opinions of different members might, and did, differ quite widely, and about which some members might, and did collect in single MSS, many different opinions. Such an arbitrary and individual matter can hardly have been the basis of group organization and practice.[1]

There has been a partial retreat from the pure form of Morton Smith's thesis. Jacob Neusner with William Scott Green and Ernest S. Frerichs edited a symposium with the title, *Judaisms and Their Messiahs at the Turn of the Christian Era* which conceded that expectations about a messiah could be the organising principle of the various groups within Judaism which they named *Judaisms*. James H. Charlesworth's Princeton Symposium, published under the title, *The Messiah: Developments in Earliest Judaism and Christianity*, published in 1992, and his own article in *Aufstieg und Niedergang der römischen Welt* in 1979, follow the same line. Since 1987 a stream of books has followed, saying much the same thing. Martin Karrer roundly asserted that

> The references to an expectation of an anointed ruler in the time just before the New Testament are confined to a few scraps of Qumran Essene literature, the Psalms of Solomon and (if it can be dated as early as this) Ethiopic Enoch 52.4 [All these things which you have seen, happen by the authority of his Messiah, so that he may give orders and be praised upon earth]. This scanty list of references, given the rich hoards of literary sources opened up from our epoch in the last few generations, cannot any longer count as an accident.[2]

He cites with full approval Charlesworth's judgment, "The 'Messiah' does not inaugurate a messianic kingdom; surprisingly, he performs no

---

[1] Smith (1959), pp. 71-72.
[2] Karrer (1990), p. 243.

functions. There is no interest in or association with a descent from David."[3] Gerbern S. Oegema finds rather more "priestly, regal or other" figures who play a liberating role in the End-time.[4] Nevertheless, whenever we find Old Testament passages being used to depict these figures in their role at the end of the days, we find such a variety of uses that we can be sure that there was no unified set of expectations. For example, "Numbers 24.17 [Balaam's prophecy that a Star would come out of Jacob and a Sceptre rise out of Israel] was connected with the expectation of a King, of a Priest-King, of a Prince, of a Teacher of the Torah, of a Warlike Messiah like Moses; as well as with God, with Claudius or with Vespasian."[5] He concludes that there was no unified idea of the Messiah, only sporadic reactions to the current tyrants or enemies of Israel, singly or in combination, which suggested, almost arbitrarily, an ideal antitype drawn from scripture;

> ...none of the biblical verses leads to a specific and uniform messianic exposition. None of the so-called proof texts from the Bible has in itself one messianic significance; the most varied verses were employed as an "inspirer" of messianic conceptions that originate from somewhere entirely different. Even the exceptions, verses that commonly bring a messianic exposition in their train (Numbers 24.17; Isaiah 11.1ff. and Daniel 7.13), support this observation.[6]

Kenneth E. Pomykala argues that "there never existed a continuous, widespread, dominant, or uniform expectation for a davidic messiah in early Judaism"; "scholarly discourse should dispense with the idea of a 'traditional' davidic hope for this period."[7] Besides the davidic messianic figure, Pomykala lists the Royal Messiahs at Qumran (the Messiah of Israel, the Prince of the Congregation, the ideal King in the "Statutes of the King" section of the Temple Scroll, the Son of God) and notes that there are texts at Qumran where David is mentioned but is not the subject of messianic speculation. He then lists the Messiah of Judah in the *Testaments of the Twelve Patriarchs*, the King of Egypt in *Sibylline Oracles* 3.286-287, the davidic messiah in *4 Ezra* who is simply the one to destroy the enemy Rome: "the function of the davidic dynasty tradition in *4 Ezra* is to aid in the characterization of the messiah as the righteous judge and destroyer of Israel's oppressor";[8]

---

[3] Karrer (1990), p.243; p. 267 note 140 for Charlesworth (1979), p. 206.
[4] Oegema (1994), p. 28; English, p. 26.
[5] Oegema, p. 302; English, p. 303.
[6] Oegema, p. 302; English, p. 303.
[7] Pomykala (1995), p. 271.
[8] Pomykala, p. 221.

and the popular messianic figures in Palestine listed by Josephus (Judas the son of Ezekias, Simon the slave of Herod, Athronges, Menachem, Simon bar Giora).

Geza Vermes's statement that "Jews of the intertestamental period, when entreating God to send the Messiah, thought of him as the son of David" is now largely swept aside by scholars who pride themselves on the sobriety of their method and their minute attention to the actual diversities of the sources.[9]

My conviction that these scholars have completely misrepresented the Judaism of the late Second Temple period is based on the observation that they do not understand how a religion works. They think that the scientific method in the study of the history of a religion depends on paying attention only to the written sources, on making as many distinctions as possible between the concepts they find recorded in the sources, on despising the beliefs of devotees of the religion as primitive and simple, and on arguing rigidly from silence that the beliefs not spoken of did not exist. The great Julius Wellhausen is their patron saint, and they despise Hermann Gunkel, his arch-enemy. Wellhausen nearly ruined Gunkel's career by his snide remark that Gunkel's *Schöpfung und Chaos* was more chaos than creation. Here are some words from Gunkel's considered reply, published in the *Expository Times* in September 1927.

> The school of Wellhausen was and still is inclined, in its constructive historical work, to be too subservient to the literary documents... It is quite possible that a thought, an incident, a conception, a turn of speech, a custom, appearing in our documents at a late period, really belongs to a much earlier age... They were disposed to pay too little heed to what has *not* come down to us in the literature. How much there is in the life and thought of an ancient people, passing from lip to lip, which never or not till quite a late period appears in the literature! All the rich content of such oral tradition must be included in our total reckoning, if that reckoning is to be accurate. The Wellhausen school follow too closely the principle, *quod non est in actis, non est in mundo* [what is not in the records does not exist], and place too much weight on the argument *ex silentio*.[10]

On our topic, the expectations about the Messiah, Gunkel asserted that "with regard to the whole christology of the New Testament, the historical person of Jesus and his impact is only *one* factor besides others:

---

[9] Vermes, (1973), p. 133.
[10] Gunkel, *ExpT*, 38 (1927), pp. 532-36 at 533-34.

indeed the main features of christology stem not from the historical Jesus, but arose independently of him and from before his time."[11]

Let us examine the case that there was no ruling messianic idea in Judaism of the late Second Temple period by drawing attention to three crucial weaknesses in it: the modern scholars' neglect of the evidence about worship, their exaggeration of the silence of the documents on the subject, and their misunderstanding of the diversity of views about the Messiah.

Everyone admits that there are scattered in our records of Judaism at the end of the Second Temple period and the century or so afterwards references to various priestly, royal or other figures who would play a liberating role in the time of the End.[12] The issue is whether these scattered references are evidence that "eschatology was, for the members of these [various] groups [in Judaism], a comparatively arbitrary and individual matter" or whether "there was some unknown higher synthesis by which these many and apparently contradictory opinions were reconciled in a single system" (to recall again Morton Smith's crucial article of 1959).[13] His challenge is clear:

> If a group had no single eschatological myth, it cannot have been organized as a community of believers in the myth it did not have. Nor can its cult acts be seen as dramatic representations of realizations of events which there was no single myth, accepted by all the members, to predict.[14]

Let us take the hint, a hint already thrown out by Vermes, and turn to the cult, to the worship of Judaism at this time. Do we find here any story embedded in the worship that would reveal to us not just isolated beliefs but a pattern of beliefs that tied together the worshippers' common reading of their past and of their present, with their common expectations of the future? Is there a story, embracing past, present and future, that has a place for a Redeemer other than the Lord God himself? If so, what was that story? What would the Messiah be like?

I call three pieces of evidence as a strong indication that there was a common story that bound worshippers together: first, the worship of the synagogue, particularly the Amidah, the prayer said standing, the prayer that was recited in one form or another at every meeting for

---

[11] Gunkel (1903), p. 64.
[12] Oegema (1994), pp. 24-28; English, pp. 21-27.
[13] Smith (1959), pp. 71-72.
[14] Smith (1959), p. 71.

worship; secondly, the Targum commonly attached to Exodus 12.42 ("this is the night of the Lord to be observed of all the children of Israel in their generations") concerning the Four Nights; and thirdly, the paintings found on the walls of the synagogue at Dura-Europos on the right bank of the Euphrates River. Each of these ties in the story of the Redeemer at the End with the past and present of the worshipping community.

The Amidah begins with three Praises that are always said. The first of these, Avoth (Fathers) blesses the God of the Fathers Abraham and Isaac and Jacob, the Most High God who remembers the pious deeds of the patriarchs and in love will bring a Redeemer to their children's children for his name's sake. The words *and in love will bring a Redeemer* are not found in the Palestinian form, but could have been suppressed because of an imperial edict. The second Benediction addresses God as the one who revives the dead. After the three Praises there follow the Intermediary Benedictions, not said on Sabbaths and Festivals, for they are petitions that need not be remembered on days of rejoicing. The Fourteenth and Fifteenth Benediction are combined in the Palestinian version, possibly again to soften the belief in a coming Redeemer.

> Be gracious, O Lord, our God, according to thy great mercies
> To Israel thy people, and Jerusalem thy city,
> And Zion, residence of thy glory;
> And to thy Temple and dwelling-place;
> And to the kingdom of the house of David, thy righteous Messiah.
> Blessed art thou, O Lord, God of David, Builder of Jerusalem.[15]

The Fourteenth and Fifteenth Benedictions according to the edition of Singer (1962) are as follows:

> And to Jerusalem, thy city, return in mercy, and dwell therein as thou hast spoken; rebuild it soon in our days as an everlasting building, and speedily set up therein the throne of David. Blessed art thou, O Lord, who rebuildest Jerusalem.
> Speedily cause the offspring [shoot] of David, thy servant, to flourish, and let his horn be exalted by thy salvation, because we wait for thy salvation all the day. Blessed art thou, O Lord, who causest the horn of salvation to flourish.

The reference to the *horn of David* is drawn from Hannah's prayer when she lent her son Samuel to the Lord at Shiloh: "the Lord shall judge the ends of the earth; and he shall give strength unto his king, and exalt the horn of his anointed" (1 Sam 2.10). The image is taken

---

[15] Vermes (1973), p. 132.

up in Psalm 132 (Remember David and all his afflictions) at verse 17, where the Lord promises, "There [in Jerusalem] will I make the horn of David to bud; I have ordained a lamp for mine anointed." In Ezekiel 29.21 it is written, "In that day I will cause the horn of the house of Israel to bud forth", another clear reference to the same tradition (yet our scholars can think that the Messiah of Israel in the Qumran writings refers to another than the Son of David).[16]

The one essential Jewish prayer refers to the Messiah, son of David, who will rebuild Jerusalem and the Temple whose worship the first David ordained for Jerusalem (1 Chron 28; 29 especially 28.1-6; cf. 1 Kings 5.3; 8.12-19; 1 Chron 6.31; 16.4; 25.1; Ezra 3.10; Ps 122). He will reign on his throne in Zion at the End.

The prayers of the congregation are at all times full of this expectation of the rebuilding of Jerusalem and the Temple and the reign of the anointed son of David. For example, at the service for the New Year they pray:

> Give then glory, O Lord, unto thy people, praise to them that fear thee, hope to them that seek thee, and free speech to them that wait for thee, joy to thy land, gladness to thy city, a flourishing horn unto David thy servant, and a clear shining light unto the son of Jesse, thine anointed, speedily in our days.[17]

The same combination of the budding horn of David and the lamp ordained for God's anointed as we found in Psalm 132.17 appears here (for the lamp, see 1 Kings 11.36; 15.4; 2 Kings 8.19; 2 Chron 21.7). Jacob Neusner, who argues that "just as there was no single 'Judaism', so...shall we look in vain for 'the Messiah myth'", has to concede that "the liturgy of the synagogue constitutes a protracted plea for the coming of the Messiah..."[18] But Judaism was united in worship, and at the centre of the most ancient services of the congregations was the hope for the coming of the Messiah, the son of Jesse, to rule in Jerusalem.

Our search is for other confirmatory evidence drawn from the worship of Judaism for a complex of themes embracing the believers' story of past present and future. We now have definite evidence that the Aramaic Targums were in existence before the destruction of the Second Temple, for fragments of Targums of Leviticus and Job have been preserved at Qumran. These Targums were paraphrases of the

---

[16] Pomykala (1995), pp. 237-39.
[17] Singer (1962), p. 328.
[18] Neusner (1984), pp. xi, 237.

Hebrew scriptures in Aramaic, the everyday language of the people. They often contained additions that explain the significance of the passages more clearly for the worshippers. In the Fragmentary Targum and the Targum Neofiti of Exodus 12.42 (or, in the ms. P of the Fragmentary Targum, to Exod 15.18, Moses' song) we have a meditation on the significance of the command to watch at night at Passover, for this same night for the Lord is one of watching for the children of Israel throughout their generations.[19]

The four nights that the worshippers are to recall as they watch on Passover night are these. The first night is the night of creation when the Word [Memra] of the Lord was revealed to the world to create it; the Word of the Lord was its light and illuminated it. The second night is the night on which the Word of the Lord revealed himself to Abram between the pieces, when he promised him a son and heir in his old age and the old age of Sarah. To our surprise this second night jumps to the night when Abraham rose up early in the morning and took Isaac to Mount Moriah to sacrifice him to the Lord.

> And Isaac was thirty-seven years old when he was offered on the altar:
> the heavens lowered themselves and bowed down
> and Isaac saw their perfections
> and his eyes were darkened by virtue of their perfections.
> And he called it the second night.

The reason for this jump is because the promise made to Abraham about Isaac seems fated to be annulled by the sacrifice of Isaac. On the contrary, it becomes the occasion when God most solemnly confirms the promise, swearing by himself (Gen 22.16-18; cf. Heb 6.13-14).

The third night is the night when the Word of the Lord manifested himself against the Egyptians at midnight; his hand slew the first-born of the Egyptians and his hand protected the first-born of Israel. The fourth night is when the End comes. Moses will emerge from the desert and the King Messiah will come from the midst of Rome. Each will march on the top of a cloud and the Word will march between the two. This is the night of the Passover when all the generations of Israel will be saved. The reference to the King Messiah coming from Rome is a sign both of his suffering and of his coming reign (*bSanh* 98a). He marches on the cloud in accordance with Dan 7.13, where one like a Son of Man will come on the clouds of heaven. He will take his throne, since, according to Rabbi Akiba, the plural *thrones were set* means One for Him and one for David (*bHagigah* 14a; *bSanhedrin* 38b).

---

[19] Levey (1974), pp. 12-13; Neusner (1984), p. 244; Le Déaut (1963).

This is confirmed by the Targum on 1 Chron 3.24 that interprets the name of the seventh son of Elioenai, one by name Anani, as the King Messiah, by a play on the word for *clouds* in Dan 7.13.[20]

Here is a complex of passages where the night of Passover is linked with creation, the birth and sacrifice of Isaac, the deliverance from Egypt, and the End when Moses and the Davidic Messiah will come, each marching on the clouds, and all generations of Israel will rise from the dead to receive the promised deliverance.

Our third example of a complex of beliefs among Jews that might give us a reliable clue to the way they saw the Messiah is in the paintings on the four walls of the synagogue at Dura Europos, painted just before AD 243-244, and mercifully preserved for us because the Romans covered the buildings close to the city wall with a mud brick embankment to fortify it against the Sassanians in AD 256. At the base of each wall is a dado less than a metre broad, and above that are three registers of panels reaching right to the ceiling. The bottom band is 1.3 metres high; the middle band 1.53 metres; and the top band 1.16 metres high. The west wall is nearly 14 metres long (13.65m), the north and south walls nearly 8 metres long (7.68m). The east wall is broken by a central door for the men and a door at the south end for the women; there are also paintings on the two sections of this east wall between the north corner and the central door, and between the central door and the women's door.

This series of paintings must represent the complex of beliefs that animated the worshippers as they gathered day by day in the synagogue. The use of paintings in synagogues may have been fairly recent, but the ideas that dictated the choice of incidents is likely to be very conservative and to represent hallowed ways of interpreting the scriptures in relation to the lives of those who worshipped there. If you are being at all daring in having paintings, you are likely to be conservative in choosing the subjects for those paintings.

Six, and six only, cycles are picked out from the Bible: Abraham sacrificing Isaac on Mount Moriah; Jacob and Joseph; Moses and Aaron; Samuel, David and Solomon, starting with Samuel and the ark, continuing with Samuel anointing David as King, David in many roles, and ending with Solomon counselling the Queen of Sheba; Elijah as the purifier of worship and the forerunner of the Messiah; and Ezekiel and the valley of dry bones.

---

[20] Levey (1974), p. 140.

Let us go into more detail. The west wall of the synagogue faced towards Jerusalem. In the centre is the niche for the Torah. To the right of the Torah shrine was a seat for the president. Above the niche is a painting labelled in Aramaic *Abraham*; this is the first of our seven cycles. The painting shows a large seven-branched candlestick, citrus fruit (the ethrog) and a palm branch (the lulah); in the centre is the Temple with four Corinthian columns. To the right is the Sacrifice of Isaac (a ram facing a small tree; Abraham with his back to the worshippers, holding a knife in his right hand; an altar with Isaac reclining on it; and a hut with a small barefooted figure turned towards the interior; and the open hand of God beside the hut). The sacrifice of Isaac, which seemed to threaten the fulfilment of God's promise to Abraham, was the most solemn moment when it was confirmed, God swearing by himself.

Then, the Jacob cycle. On the north wall in the top register nearest the Torah shrine is Jacob reclining with his head on the stone. Angels are ascending the ladder that rests on the stone. Also in the top register, but in the centre of the west wall above the Torah shrine is a picture perhaps of Joseph, with two attendants, revealing himself to his eleven brothers in Egypt. In the middle register below, Jacob is blessing his sons and to the north Joseph presents his two sons Manasseh and Ephraim to Jacob to bless, and presumably it shows Jacob contradicting Joseph and saying that the younger will be the greater (Gen 48.5-22). Perhaps the mysterious panel in the middle register of the south wall is a picture of Joseph's bones being carried from Egypt towards the Promised Land.[21] If so, this would link the Joseph cycle with the Moses and Aaron cycle.

The third cycle, on Moses, consists of five or six panels. The finding of Moses by Pharaoh's daughter and her committing her through Miriam to his mother is a prominent panel at the right of the west wall. In the north wing of the central panels, the top register, there is a picture of Moses at the burning bush, his shoes standing beside him. Next to that on the north side is a large and impressive panel of the Exodus, showing Moses three times: cleaving the Red Sea, holding back the waters, and sweetening the pool of Marah with his rod. The Israelites are shown twice, marching into the sea in filthy garments, and marching out of the sea in shining clean garments. In the middle register of the west wall, but at the south end is the magnificent panel showing Moses smiting the rock with his rod. Twelve rivers flow from

---

[21] Wischnitzer (1948), pp. 53-55.

the rock, each flowing to a tent at the door of each of which stands the representative of the twelve tribes. (The LXX of Psalm 104 [105].41 preserves the tradition that ποταμοί/rivers ran in the dry places.) To the north of this panel, nearer the Torah shrine, is a large panel of Aaron and priests preparing to sacrifice. On the north side is a striking panel of an old man with the sun, the moon and seven stars above his head. Perhaps this represents the day on which Joshua commanded the sun and the moon and the stars to stand still upon Gibeon (Josh 10.12-13).[22]

The fourth cycle begins with Samuel. This fourth cycle has more pictures than any other. In the middle register at the east end of the north wall only the bottom of the picture has survived, but it is likely to be Hannah presenting Samuel before the shrine at Shiloh. We have already seen how important her prayer on that occasion was, with the prophecy that the Lord would give strength to his king and exalt the horn of his anointed (1 Sam 2.10). Moving in the same register towards the west we have in turn the Battle of Eben Ezer, the capture of the ark by the Philistines. Turning the corner, in the same register on the west wall there is a dramatic representation of the havoc wrought by the presence of the ark in the Temple of Dagon and a picture of the ark being sent back on a special cart drawn by two kine. Perhaps the impressive figure reading from a scroll in the middle register of the west wall directly below Moses and the burning bush is Samuel, although I wonder if it is not Josiah reading the scroll found when the Temple was being restored (2 Kings 23.2; 2 Chron 34.30).

Samuel then appears anointing David the youngest son of Jesse. This panel occupies the prominent position on the west wall just to the right of the Torah shrine and behind the seat of the president. On the east wall, between the men's entrance and the north wall, perhaps we have a panel depicting David sparing Saul, but it is hard to decipher.

Clear, and much more important, David as king seated and playing his harp with a lion and a dove at his feet occupies the top of the central panel immediately above the Torah shrine and the painting of the sacrifice of Isaac. The remainder of this panel is devoted to Jacob's blessing of his twelve sons and Jacob's blessing of Joseph's two sons which we have already mentioned. In the top register of this west wall, balancing the panel of Moses at the burning bush, is another figure, dressed differently from Moses, but also with his shoes standing

---

[22] E.L. Sukenik (1934), p. 84.

empty besides his feet. Unfortunately his head has been lost. The only other prominent incident of someone important going barefoot up a mount is King David going up the ascent of Olivet weeping as he went with his head covered; this was when he was forced to flee from Jerusalem at the rebellion of Absalom (2 Sam 15.30; the panel is unlikely to depict Isaiah going barefoot, Isa 20.2, 4). Immediately to the south of this panel is one labelled Solomon. He is seated on the throne with alternate lions and eagles crouching (Targum Sheni to Esther).[23] There is a Greek inscription συνκάθαδρος, which here cannot mean *assessor* but must mean that he is engaged in offering counsel to an equal; the two are in conference. The female figure is probably, then, the Queen of Sheba. Since one of the patrons of the synagogue was a proselyte, this would be an appropriate incident to portray on the wall. Perhaps Solomon's temple also appears at the culmination of the ark sequence, in the middle register of the west wall. It contains a gate showing pagan-looking figures: two bulls, two large naked men each with two smaller men, and two clothed women with cornucopias and rudders. Perhaps this is a gate by which the Gentiles might enter the true Temple.

The fifth cycle is the Elijah cycle. Starting with the east wall, between the men's entrance and the women's perhaps we have Elijah fed by the ravens. There is no doubt that the south wall, reading from the left, shows Elijah and the widow of Zarephath gathering sticks to make her last meal; the vain attempt by the prophets of Baal to offer a sacrifice, their trick of having a man hidden inside the altar to light the fire being shown frustrated by a large snake biting him; and at the corner, Elijah's sacrifice. Around the corner on the west wall still in the lowest register we have Elijah raising the widow's son from death. I am inclined to agree with Rachel Wischnitzer that a large and prominent panel I have not previously mentioned, the story of Esther, could well belong in the Elijah cycle. The Esther panel, in the lowest register of the west wall immediately to the left of the Torah shrine, shows, reading from the worshippers' right to left, Esther on her throne, Esther having left her throne to intercede for her people to King Ahasuerus and his granting her request, counsellors denouncing Haman, and on the extreme left, Haman leading Mordecai mounted on the king's horse and gloriously arrayed. Wischnitzer noticed that the counsellor nearest to Haman and Mordecai has a fringe sewn at the hem of his garment such as pious Jews wore, and she conjectured that

---

[23] Wischnitzer (1948), p. 113 n. 7.

this is the counsellor Harbonah (Esther 7.9) whom Jewish legend said was Elijah in disguise (*Esther Rabbah* 7.9).[24]

The sixth cycle is the whole lowest register of the north wall, Ezekiel and the valley of dry bones. The end nearest the door has remained something of a mystery. I think it perhaps shows the prophet Ezekiel dressed for killing work wielding a sword against the apostate Jews, one of whom is seen kneeling at the behest of a soldier dressed in Roman armour at a pagan altar (for the altar contains a small idol).[25] The prophet Ezekiel was commanded by God to smite idolaters with a sword (Ezek 6.11-14; 21.8-17) and so is responsible for the valley of dry bones. Moving towards the west, the panel shows God's arm stretched out to command Ezekiel to raise the dead. Ezekiel is shown twice, once with the ten tribes lifting their hands in prayer, and again, commanding the four winds to raise the dead. There are thirteen dismembered bodies lying waiting to be raised. Then, nearer the corner, comes a lay figure in a most elaborate tunic, whom Rachel Wischnitzer and Kraeling identify as King David. To his right, on the other side of more dead bodies, are figures representing Judah (with God's hand touching his head) and Benjamin and Ephraim (for the ten tribes beyond Euphrates are really nine plus the half-tribe of Manasseh, *2 Bar* 78.1 [cf. *4 Ezra* 13.40; Josephus *Antiquities* 11.133; *mSanh* 10.3]). David is prominent because of the verse in Ezekiel 37 that says, "And David my servant shall be king over them; and they all shall have one shepherd: they shall also walk in my judgments, and observe my statutes, and do them" (Ezek 37.24). All the tribes will return to the Promised Land.

Paul Flesher has recently challenged the view that Dura's Jews held messianism as a key belief; he argued that "far from being a key belief, a messiah remains relatively unimportant at Dura."[26] He very helpfully uses computer enhancement of the picture of David seated playing a harp. He shows that he has a shepherd's crook on his right and that the figures at his feet are a lion and a dove, thus disposing of the idea that David is pictured like Orpheus. However, the case for the messianic interpretation of the paintings does not stand or fall with this identification. Flesher is right that David indicates the national unity of the Jewish people, but he does not seem to understand that this unity was also seen as a future promise when a son of David would again reign over a reunited people. He does not ask himself why Elijah is so

---

[24] Wischnitzer, p. 32.
[25] Hopkins (1979), p. 171.
[26] Flesher (1995), p. 366.

prominent—having four or five separate panels devoted to him. He lacks understanding of synagogue worship. In this synagogue the worshippers gathered to hear the Law read, an occasion when they were reminded of their sins and given the opportunity to repent. Abraham is shown in obedience offering Isaac, who submits meekly to his destiny; Jacob dreams of the angels carrying his prayers to heaven and returning with answers; Joseph reveals himself in mercy to his brothers who had sold him into slavery; Moses leads out a filthy people from Egypt and cleanses them in the Sea of Reeds and gives them sweet water to drink; Samuel is given to Eli to replace Eli's sinful sons and to comfort the people when the ark is captured by the Philistines as a sign of their sinfulness; David in exile climbs Olivet barefoot and weeping; Elijah almost alone faces down an apostate people who have gone after Baal; and Ezekiel raises a people who are slain because of their sin.

Each of the six cycles contains hope for sinners. God provides a ram for the sacrifice instead of Isaac; Jacob blesses his sons and the two sons of Joseph, promising great things to come; Joseph's bones are carried from Egypt to Canaan (perhaps); Moses is not killed but found by Pharaoh's daughter; God reveals himself to Moses at the burning bush; he leads the people out of Egypt; Aaron his brother is consecrated High Priest; Samuel anoints David; David is portrayed as the shepherd king playing on the harp to drive away evil, accompanied by the lion of sovereignty and the dove of peace; Solomon builds the Temple and is consulted by the Queen of Sheba; Elijah is the prophet who is to announce the great and dreadful day of the Lord (Mal 4.5-6; LXX 3.23-24); he is, according to the Targum Pseudo-Jonathan to Exod 40.10, the High Priest who is to be sent at the end of the dispersions. Just as Elijah raised the dead, so God will raise the dead of Israel in the valley of dry bones and bring them back to the Promised Land where David will reign over the reunited tribes.

Many scenes, one set of themes; one Messiah, the son of David.

Few scholars are as tone-deaf to worship as Flesher. Scholars like Jacob Neusner who deny that there was a set of messianic beliefs common to Judaism fully admit the force of this evidence from worship, but they argue that these messianic themes were simply inert traditional motifs that were passed on mechanically in the Mishnah, for example, and did not represent the living ideology of the rabbis in the second century: "to the system of the Mishna, the messiah theme is inert, indeed, useless."[27] George Foot Moore and Morton Smith and all his followers emphasize the sparsity of messianic references in the great mass of literature now available to us, the contradictoriness of the images of the End, and the mutiplicity of figures who play a role in the final salvation. Scholars now tend to make almost every corpus of literature represent a separate and distinct Judaism and to deny any community of messianic themes.

There is another way of reading this sort of evidence. The sparsity of literary references to the Messiah may be the usual reticence about beliefs that are fundamental and basic. The allegedly contradictory pictures of the End may be the result of scholarly attempts to unpick intricate patterns of belief in order to posit simple and distinct origins for them. For example, it is commonly argued that the belief that the dead will be sorted out into the righteous and the unrighteous at death contradicts and has a different origin from the belief that the dead will be raised and finally judged in their risen bodies. However, both beliefs are found in the same documents (for example, in *4 Ezra*), so that the compilers did not think they were incompatible.[28] Finally, the atomistic reading of the documents so that they can be made to refer to disparate redemptive figures may have overlooked the web of connection and allusion that binds all the figures together and connects them all to the one supreme Messiah, the son of David.

The three examples of systems of worship that each show a lively interest in the coming Davidic Messiah, the Amidah, the song of the four nights, and the synagogue paintings at Dura-Europos, all suggest that the second way of reading the literary evidence that I propose is likely to be more faithful to the living Judaism of the century before and after the destruction of the Second Temple.

I am not arguing for an agreed detailed system, but for a core belief that was the basis of all further speculation, "messianic hope" which had "a relatively stable core", to use the words of William Horbury.[29] If people could ask what the Messiah would be like, there was plenty of room for argument and disagreement. Scripture gave clues and hints, but all were free to interpret the prophecies as best they could. Here is my central thesis in this chapter. The Messiah the son of David would come at the End incognito, pursued and harassed as the first David was by Saul and, later in the time of exile from Jerusalem, by

---

[27] Neusner (1993), p. 300.
[28] Reiser (1990) and my review, O'Neill (1993a).
[29] Horbury (1985), p. 38; cf. pp. 39-40, 48-52; (1998), chapter III, "The Coherence of Messianism."

Absalom his favourite son who led a revolt against him. The Messiah was forbidden to say in so many words who he was. This was a time for everyone to repent. Unfortunately, it was quite possible that someone whom many thought was the Messiah was an imposter, an agent of Satan, the Antichrist, who would deceive Israel. Everyone who was looking for the Messiah searched the scriptures for clues as to what he would be like. Many other figures besides David were drawn upon as types of the Messiah, but each clue was related to the Messiah son of David. In short, I wish to argue that there was a clear common set of doctrines about the coming Messiah, but plenty of room for discussion and argument about whether the Messiah had already come or not. All the literary evidence, I argue, supports and is congruent with that set of theses.

I shall first show that two messianic passages from the Law and one from the Former Prophets were picked up in the Later Prophets and the Writings. These three passages are often referred to, and treated as a messianic corpus in the Later Prophets and in the Writings, particularly the Psalms. This corpus was alive in the minds of leaders and people in Second Temple Judaism so that allusions to the core three passages from the Law and the Former Prophets commonly turn up whenever the future hopes of Israel are being discussed. After dealing briefly with the charge that messianism is an inert and unimportant belief in the Mishnah, I shall then show that many of the Jewish writings that are alleged to contain no reference to the Messiah in fact contain clear enough allusions to one or more of these passages. I shall then deal with some passages that are alleged, in referring to a Messiah not the son of David, to represent a non-davidic messianism.

I shall then try to show that everyone agreed that the Messiah at his first appearance would be unknown, and hard to recognize.

I shall also try to show that the Messiah was expected to suffer and even to die before the coming of the End.

The Messianic Core of three passages from the Law and the Former Prophets assumed in the Bible

There are two pivotal messianic passages in the Torah: the blessing on Judah in the Blessings of Jacob, Gen 49.8-12, and Balaam's prophecy in Num 24.

Gen 49.10 reads, "The sceptre shall not depart from Judah, nor a lawgiver from between his feet, until Shiloh come; and unto him shall the gathering of the people (or, in the LXX, of the nations) be." Judah is typified as the lion. Num 24.17 reads, "There shall come a Star out of Jacob, and a Sceptre shall rise out of Israel, and shall smite the corners of Moab, and destroy all the children of Sheth"; Balaam earlier referred to the great king (Num 24.7) who is a lion (Num 24.9), and of course the word *sceptre* binds the two passages together.

The third passage is found in the Former Prophets. Nathan promised David in the name of the Lord that after David's death God would set up David's seed after him and would establish his kingdom. David's seed would build a house for God's name. "I will be his father, and he shall be my son." "And thine house and thy kingdom shall be established for ever before thee: thy throne shall be established for ever." Nathan's prophecy here in 2 Sam 7.12-16 (cf. 1 Chron 17.11-14) was taken as showing that the king who was promised in the Blessings of Jacob and in Balaam's prophecy, the king who would reign over the nations, would be David's son; the eternity of the kingdom of David was taken as an indication that the prophecy was not simply a prophecy about Solomon. A kingdom that was established for ever would be proof against any enemy; this king would implicitly rule the nations, for God would set up his throne for ever. The passage brought out a special feature of the set of beliefs, namely, that God would call his anointed one *Son* and he would call God *Father*.

These three passages in turn were taken up by the writing prophets, most notably in Isaiah chapter 11, but pervasively in almost all of them, and by the Psalms. Gen 49, the Blessing of Judah, is cited or alluded to in the Psalms (his hand will be on the neck of his enemies, Ps 18.40; Judah is my lawgiver, Ps 60.7; 108.8); the theme of waiting until he come is echoed in Isa 11.1; 62.11; Ezek 21.27; Dan 9.25; and the theme of the gathering of the people with the conquest of the nations is prominent in Isaiah (Isa 2.2; 11.10; 42.1-2, 4; 49.6-7, 22-23; 55.4-5; 60.1-5), is found in Haggai (Hag 2.7) and pervades all visions of the End.

Num 24, Balaam's prophecy, refers specifically to Jacob's blessing of Judah: "out of Jacob shall come he that hath dominion" (Num 24.19). It speaks of a king whose kingdom will be exalted (Num 24.7), who is a lion (Num 24.9), and who will have Edom as a possession (Num 24.18). He will break his enemies' bones (Num 24.7), as the son will do in Ps 2.9, and his arrows will pierce his enemies, as the arrows of the king in Ps 45.5. The LXX of the obscure beginning of this seventh verse, "He shall pour the water out of his buckets, and his seed shall be in many waters", reads, "A man shall come of his seed and he will rule many nations." Similarly, the LXX renders "there shall come a Star out of Jacob, and a Sceptre shall rise out of Israel" as "there shall rise a star out of Jacob and there shall arise a man out of Israel." The term *man* has clear messianic associations in the Prophets and the Writings, as Vermes and Horbury have abundantly shown.[30] He is called *Sceptre*, and in the Psalms David's son is said to wield a sceptre (Ps 45.7; cf. 23.4). The term *star* was not taken up in the Bible because Balaam might have been thought of as seeing this king as just one star among many (cf. Amos 5.26; Isa 14.12), but Malachi speaks of the ruling body in the heavens, the sun, as the one who will come at the End: "the Sun of righteousness shall arise with healing in his wings" (Mal 4.2; LXX 3.20). In the Psalms, with reference to Nathan's prophecy in 2 Sam 7, David's throne is said to endure as the sun that rules the day and as the moon that rules the night before the Lord (Ps 89.36-37).

Nathan's prophecy to David in 2 Sam 7 forms the basis of Psalm 89, being cited time and time again (Ps 89.4, 26, 27, 29, 34, 36, 37). The phrase "the fruit of thy body will I set upon thy throne" in Ps 132.11 comes straight out of 2 Sam 7. The promise that the Messiah will call God *Father*, and God call the Messiah *Son* is cited in Ps 89.26-27 and alluded to in Psalm 2. Jeremiah emphasizes that God's covenant with his people is as unalterable as his promise to David in 2 Sam 7 (Jer 33.21). The prophecy that David's son would build a house is picked up in Amos 9.11: "in that day will I raise up the tabernacle of David that is fallen...", which also alludes to Num 24 and Gen 49 in the words, "that they may possess the remnant of Edom, and of all the heathen, which are called by my name" (Amos 9.12).

The all-pervasiveness of this set of beliefs founded on just three prophecies in the Law and Former Prophets is still widely denied. Morton Smith, for example, writes that "many Old Testament prophecies of the coming kingdom or world have no messiah." He assumes that the collections in which these prophecies are embedded cannot be thought of as belonging to an agreed system. He mentions Ezekiel chapters 38 and 39, forgetting to mention that chapter 37, the valley of dry bones, so graphically depicted on the north wall of the synagogue at Dura-Europos, makes an explicit prophecy that David my servant will be king over the resurrected tribes of Israel (Ezek 37.24).

E.P. Sanders says that "the expectation of a messiah was not the rule" in late Second Temple Judaism; he concedes that there "a few clear biblical passages", citing Jer 23.5-6 and Isa 9.7 as the most

---

[30] Vermes (1961), pp. 159-60; Horbury (1985), pp. 49-52.

famous, but he asserts that "the hope is missing from important sections of the prophetic corpus (such as Isa 40-66)..."[31] The two passages he cites are both referring back to the prophecies about the king to come mentioned in Gen 49 and Num 24 who will be David's son according to 2 Sam 7. The branch theme in his Jeremiah passage is found frequently, in various forms, in Isaiah and Zechariah (Isa 4.2; Jer 33.15; Zech 6.12-13; Isa 11.1). The fact that Zechariah thought that Joshua the son of Josedech the high priest was the man whose name is the Branch subsumes Joshua under the Davidic promises and does not in any way change them. Of the Writing Prophets, Isaiah, Jeremiah, Ezekiel, Hosea and Amos mention the name David with reference to the coming king. Those that do not explicitly name David refer to the three Davidic prophecies in one way or another: Daniel speaks of the kingdom that will never be destroyed (Dan 2.44; 4.3; 6.26); Joel refers to the three prophecies by saying, "for in mount Zion and in Jerusalem shall be deliverance, as the Lord hath said, and in the remnant whom the Lord shall call" (2.32), a theme picked up in Obadiah 17, and his statement that "Judah shall dwell for ever" is a pretty clear reference to Gen 49 (Joel 3.18-20); Jonah in the belly of the fish prays a catena drawn from the Psalms of David; Micah prophesies, "Assemble Jacob as sheep; their king shall pass before them", a clear reference to David the shepherd king (cf. Hos 3.5), and he says that the saviour will come from Bethlehem of Judah (Mic 5.2-3); Nahum's call to "behold upon the mountains the feet of him that bringeth good tidings, that publisheth peace" is probably a reference to David's son who will come to Zion and bring peace (Nah 1.15; Isa 61.1; cf. Isa 52.7); Hab 2.14 cites Isa 11.9, "For the earth shall be filled with the knowledge of the glory of the Lord, as the waters cover the sea", and Isa 11 is a clear passage about the Davidic Messiah; Zephaniah emphasizes that the Lord will be in the midst as King of Israel, but the Davidic shepherd imagery is found in reference to the righteous remnant who will feed and lie down and none shall make them afraid (Zeph 3.13); Haggai sees in Zerubbabel the governor of Judah, who will rebuild the Lord's house, one like a signet, the chosen one, messianic attributes drawn from the Messianic Song of Songs and Isaiah with their reference to the judgment of the Gentiles (Songs 8.6; Isa 42.1; 43.10); and in Malachi there is the reference to the burning Sun of righteousness already mentioned in discussing the Star of Jacob (Mal 4.2; LXX 3.26; Num 24).

---

[31] Sanders (1992), pp. 295-306. But see Isa 40.11; 42.4; 55.3, 4.

Sanders leaves out of account the Psalms, many of which are specifically linked to David.

Attempts to show that these Messianic Core passages were not alive and not important in late Second Temple Judaism and shortly after

Let us leave the Bible proper and see whether this complex of ideas about the coming in David's greater son was or was not important in the Jewish literature of the century or so before the destruction of the Second Temple and the century or so after. Sanders is repeating a common view when he asserts that "there are relatively few—strikingly few—references to a Davidic king in the literature of our period."[32]

On the contrary, the three passages I have argued formed an agreed core of prophecies about the coming salvation (Gen 49; Num 24; 2 Sam 7) are important as forming part of a system in Judaism at the turn of the era.

Gen 49.10 is cited in the Patriarchal Blessings in 4Q252, and explicitly linked with Jer 23.5; 33.15,17; Zech 3.8; 6.12, all mentioning David. Targum Onkelos takes the passage as messianic. Joshua cites Gen 49.10 in Pseudo-Philo's *Biblical Antiquities*, a book that modern scholars quite mistakenly think is not about the Davidic Messiah (21.5).[33] The Blessing of Jacob at the centre of the west wall of the synagogue at Dura-Europos is dominated by David sitting enthroned, with a crook in his right hand and a harp in his left hand, and a lion and a dove at his feet. Gen 49.10 is cited and interpreted in 4Q Patriarchal Blessings (4Q252 5): "Whenever Israel rules, there shall not fail to be a descendant of David upon the throne ... until the Messiah of righteousness comes, the Branch of David." Yet Pomykala thinks that Gen 49.10 is one of the "non-davidic Royal Traditions" and that the *Testaments of the Twelve Patriarchs* refer to a Messiah of Judah distinct from the Davidic Messiah.[34] He concedes that *TJud* 24 combines references to Gen 49 with references to Isa 11, a clearly Davidic passage, and he overlooks the references to Num 24. Then he disposes of the evidence as appearing to be from the pen of a Christian writer.[35] He concedes that *TJud* 22 is closely based on Gen 49 and contains echoes

---

[32] Sanders (1992), p. 296.
[33] O'Neill (1994a).
[34] Pomykala (1995), pp. 23-24; 246-55. Vermes (1995), p. 302. Horbury (1998a), pp. 11, 50, 66.
[35] Pomykala (1995), p. 252.

of other Davidic passages, particularly 2 Sam 7. Nevertheless he persists in labelling the Messiah of Judah as a specific non-davidic Messiah. His whole case is flawed by the anachronistic assumption that any Jew of the time could have conceived of a Messiah from the tribe of Judah who was not the son of David.

Num 24 appears frequently in later Jewish literature in contexts referring to the davidic Messiah. Num 24.17 is cited in the Damascus Document 7.19-20 and in the same context is quoted Amos 9.11, "I will raise up the tabernacle of David that is fallen." In the *Testament of Levi*, a priest at the End is said to arise as a star in heaven, but this is no priestly Messiah but a Messiah who is both priest and king: his star will arise from heaven *as a king* (*TLevi* 18.3). A few verses later it is said that the knowledge of the Lord will be poured out on earth as the water of lakes, a clear reference to Isa 11.9, a Davidic Messiah passage (*TLevi* 18.5). The messianic passage in the *Testament of Judah* 24 already discussed with reference to Gen 49 begins with a reference to Num 24.17 and later, in verse 5, alludes to the *sceptre of my kingdom* (also an allusion to Gen 49.10). It contains a clear reference to Isa 11.1 in the words *from your root a stem will grow and in him will a rod of righteousness arise for the nations* (*TJud* 24.5-6), and Isa 11.1 is about a rod out of the stem of Jesse, the Davidic messiah. The Targums of Numbers take the passage as referring to the King Messiah, that is, the Messiah of David.

In 2 Sam 7.14 and 1 Chron 17.13 it is said that God would be Father to the one who would be his Son, the descendant of David. The ruling opinion, backed by the combined authority of Bultmann and Jeremias, that *Son of God* was not a title for the Messiah at the time of the New Testament, depended in part in Origen's round assertion that the Jews he knew could not use the term *Son of God* in the way Celsus's alleged Jewish informant was supposed to have done by saying, "But my prophet said once in Jerusalem that God's son would come to judge..." (Origen, *Contra Celsum* 1.49; 4.2). We now are more confident that Celsus's Jew was well informed and can be trusted. Nathan's prophecy has been picked up in the Bible itself, in Psalm 2.7 and Psalm 89.27-28; the words of the prophecy are cited and explicitly related to the branch of David and linked with the prophecy in Amos 9.11 about God's raising up the hut of David which has fallen in 4Q Florilegium (4Q174 1.10-13); and they are alluded to in the reference to the time when God would beget his Messiah among them in 1QSa (1Q28a) 2.11-12. The Aramaic fragment 4Q246 speaks of a warrior who will be called son of God and son of the Most High, a great God among the gods. The term *Son of God* is found in Philo, the *Testaments* of the Twelve Patriarchs, 4 Baruch, 1 Enoch, 4 Ezra and 5 Ezra.[36] All these passages draw on the prophecy of Nathan to David; the title *Son of God* was an established title for the son of David who would be revealed at the end, and this is clinched by 4QFlorilegium.

Another theme in 2 Sam 7, the promise that David's son would reign for ever, is a commonplace in visions of the End. For example, in *SibOr* 3.286-290, it is said that "the God of heaven shall send a king, and shall judge each man with blood and flame of fire. There is a royal tribe, whose family shall never stumble: and this in the circuit of times shall have dominion and shall begin to raise up a new shrine of God."[37] This third book of the *Sibylline Oracles* concludes with a picture of the peace and harmony of the new age drawn from Isa 11, clearly Davidic.

The Alleged Scarcity of References to the Davidic Messiah

Perhaps I have succeeded in convincing you that the three key passages from Gen 49, Num 24 and 2 Samuel 7 were often quoted and alluded to in the rest of the Bible and in Jewish writings. How am I to answer the charge that the expectation of a Davidic King appears but seldom in the literature, and that in most of the writings God alone brings in his kingdom or his agents are other than a son of David?

The charge that the Davidic Messiah appears but seldom in the texts rests on two errors. First, scholars will only accept a passage as Davidic if the word *David* occurs, overlooking the rich set of symbols, based primarily on Gen 49, Num 24 and 2 Sam 7, that would suggest to any worshipper familiar with the Bible that David is referred to: symbols such as shepherd (*1 Enoch* 90.29; *5 Ezra* 2.34), vine (Targum Pseudo-Jonathan to Gen 9.20; *2 Baruch* 39.7; cf. *3 Baruch* 4.8-17; cf. *Didache* 9.2), lion (*4 Ezra* 11.37; *TJoseph* 19), the righteous one (Jer 23.5-6; Tobit 13.6; *2 Enoch* 72.6) who will sit on a throne (Sir 47.11; *1 Enoch* 62.3; *Jubilees* 31.18-20; 1 Macc 2.57). The very terms *Zion* or *Jerusalem* immediately suggested the Davidic King, for Jerusalem is the City of David (2 Sam 5.9; 6.12, 16; 1 Kings 2.10; 3.1; 8.1; 9.24 &c.).

Secondly, modern scholars are tending to treat the texts as though they were modern books written by single authors. They assume that a theme that happens to be mentioned only once is not important in the system of beliefs of the author. But these ancient books are not written

---

[36] For a full list of passages see O'Neill (1988), pp. 485-86.
[37] Translated by Lanchester in Charles (1913), p. 384.

What Would the Messiah Be Like? 49

by single authors; they are collections of sacred traditions, and each tradition has a part to play in the intricate system of beliefs of communities. What happens to be mentioned only once may be an essential part of the whole. The observance by the early Christians of the first day of the week as the day of corporate public worship is scarcely recorded in the New Testament (as Basil Hall pointed out to me long ago). It is not the documents that should determine our view of the ancient religious practices, but the ancient religious practices, which are inherently conservative, that should show us how to read the documents. It is only by overlooking all the many allusions to David and by expecting the key role of David to be represented by long and central discussions, as though these ancient collections were modern books, that modern scholars can make such assertions as that the Davidic king "plays a key role only in Ps Sol 17."[38]

For an example of the distortions produced by this way of reading documents, let us take the case of Jubilees. Oegema quotes with evident satisfaction R.H. Charles as saying, "Although our author [of *Jubilees*] is an upholder of the Maccabean dynasty he still clings...to the hope of a messiah sprung from Judah. He makes, however, only once reference to this Messiah, and no role of any importance is assigned to him."[39]

Morton Smith even asserted that there is no Messiah in Jubilees, certainly not in the prophecy of the coming age in chapter 23. But he, and Charles before him, and Oegema after him underestimate the messianic import of the overthrow of Satan and of the assertion that the Lord will heal his servants and they will see great peace (verses 29-30), precisely the things David will do: conquer enemies and heal, as did the first David by shepherding his sheep and by playing on his harp. The clear reference to the blessings on Levi and Judah in chapter 31 are dismissed as "on the verge of messianism": where Judah is to be a prince over the sons of Jacob who will tread down all who hate him, before whom the Gentiles will fear and all nations quake, who will sit on a throne and who will bring peace to the sons of the Beloved (*Jubilees* 31.18-20). All the clear echoes of Jacob's blessing of Judah in Gen 49.8-12 are ignored; the imagery of Balaam's unwilling prophecy in Numbers 24 about the Jewish king, called Star and Sceptre (itself a cross-reference to Gen 49) is ignored. The brevity of the references is

---

[38] Sanders (1992), p. 296.
[39] Charles (1902), p. lxxxvii; Oegema (1994), p. 58, note 97; English p. 57, note 96.

taken as infallible proof of their lack of importance in the religious system of the community that treasured these traditions.

Morton Smith also thinks there is no Messiah in *2 Enoch* (the *Slavonic Enoch*). He overlooked the Righteous One after the order of Melchizedek who is both priest and king in Salem, David's city (*2 En* 72.6). The Melchizedek passage has already in Psalm 110 been applied to David's greater son, whom David calls *Lord*.

On the grounds of the scarcity of reference and the alleged contrast in world-view of the regulations in the Mishnah and the messianic frame of mind, Neusner has asserted that the Messiah in the Mishnah was simply an inert and useless part of the system.[40] "For the philosophers of the Mishnah the Messiah figure presents no rich resource of myth or symbol. The Messiah forms part of the inherited, but essentially undifferentiated, background of factual material. The figure is neither to be neglected nor to be exploited."[41] Here is the modern fallacy of treating collections as artificial treatises by authors with a conscious ideology. The Mishnah is not the work of philosophers; it is a collection of legal rulings. "The genre of the Mishna precludes the need for Messianic reference..."[42] But the Messianic assumption is clearly there, as Neusner concedes: "the Messiah forms part of the inherited...background of factual materials."[43] The Mishnah is collected in order to preserve the teachings of the guardians of the unwritten Law to show Israel how to find holiness in the observance of the commandments. Why? So that they would be able to stand as righteous in the presence of the Messiah. A key part of belief was the expectation that, when Israel kept the Law, the Messiah would come and their dispersion and captivity would be over (Daniel 9.4-19; *TJudah* 23.5; cf. 24.1ff.; *TDan* 6.4; *Jubilees* 1.15-17, 23; *Assumption of Moses* 1.18; Baruch 4.28-37; *2 Baruch* 78.6,7; cf. Acts 3.19-21).

In fact the one or two casual references to the Messiah show that it is not true that "To the system of the Mishna, the messiah theme is inert, indeed, useless."[44]

The first casual reference is in *Berakoth* 1.5. The legal issue is the recitation of the section of the Shema concerning Fringes (Num 15.37-41) at night. Fringes were only worn during the day, not at night, for at night the light was lacking by which "to look upon it"

---

[40] Neusner (1993), p. 300.
[41] Neusner (1984), p. 30.
[42] Dr Sacha Stern, Jews' College, London, in a private letter, 18 June 1998.
[43] Neusner (1984), p. 30.
[44] Neusner (1993), p. 300.

[Num 15.39]). R. Eleazar b. Azariah (a rabbi of the second generation) confessed that all his life he had failed to prove it until he learnt the reason from a young colleague, Ben Zoma (of the third generation). Ben Zoma drew attention to Deut 16.3, the command to remember the day of exodus from Egypt *all the days of thy life*. The little word *all* signified the nights also.

Although Ben Zoma's proof of the reason for reciting the Shema at night was accepted, his further argument, that the Shema would not be recited in the days of the Messiah (based on Jer 23.7-8), was rejected. The Sages appealed to the same verse as Ben Zoma had used to justify saying the section of the Shema on Fringes at night to support the position that the Shema would still be recited in the days of the messiah: "*all* the days" included the days of the Messiah. The fact that this reference to the Messiah in the Mishnah is entirely subordinate to a dispute about why the section of the Shema on Fringes was to be recited at night shows, paradoxically enough, how central was the belief that the days of the Messiah were longingly expected. The point of keeping the Law was to be ready for the days of the Messiah. The Messiah is almost never mentioned in the Mishnah because every legal requirement was fulfilled to please the Lord in the hope that he would at last send the Messiah.

Seemingly casually, in another passage, the Mishnah echoes the daily prayers in the synagogue: "There was no happier days for Israel than the 15th of Ab and the Day of Atonement... It saith, Go forth ye daughters of Sion, and behold king Solomon with the crown wherewith his mother hath crowned him in the day of his espousals and in the day of the gladness of his heart (Song of Songs 3.11). In the day of his espousals—this is the giving of the Law; and in the day of the gladness of his heart—this is the building of the Temple. May it be built speedily, in our days!" (*m.Taanith* 4.8). Solomon of the Song of Songs stands for David's son, the Messiah, who will rebuild the Temple, according to 2 Sam 7. (Karrer thinks that there is absolutely no reference to the messianic Son of David in the Mishnah.)[45]

We cannot leave the Mishnah without a note on the concluding paragraphs of *Sotar* 9, after the sad list of the last great rabbis, beginning, When R. Meir died there were no more makers of parables, and ending, When Rabbi died humility and the shunning of sin ceased. These concluding paragraphs are not part of the Mishnah and are commented upon neither by Moses Maimonides nor by Obadiah of

---

[45] Karrer (1990), p. 269.

Bertinoro.[46] The late rabbis who inserted these paraagraphs took the sad progressive decline of virtue with the death of their great forebears as "footprints of the Messiah": the wisdom of the Scribes shall become insipid and the truth shall nowhere be found; children shall shame the elders and the disorder foretold in Micah 7.6 will come to pass. The phrase "footprints of the Messiah" is an allusion to the messianic Psalm 89 (verses 49-52), which itself cites and alludes to 2 Sam 7.12-16 several times (Ps 89.3, 4, 20-37). Since the same theme of the footprints of the Messiah is picked up by Josephus in his phrase "the signs of salvation", the motif can confidently be dated as important before the Fall of Jerusalem (Josephus, *War* 2.259; 6.285).

Neusner gives us this translation of the Mishnah *Sotar* 9.15:

> Pinhas b. Yair says, "Heedfulness leads to cleanliness, cleanliness leads to cleanness, cleanness leads to abstinence, abstinence leads to holiness, holiness leads to modesty, modesty leads to the fear of sin, the fear of sin leads to piety, piety leads to the Holy Spirit, the Holy Spirit leads to the resurrection of the dead, and the resurrection of the dead comes through Elijah, blessed be his memory. Amen."[47]

The whole point of this saying, lying at the end of a long series of descriptions of the corruption of the age, is that only by the pursuit of a holy observance of the Law can Jews be ready to greet the Messiah when he comes.

The very fact of the existence of the Mishnah is a plea to stand against the corruption of the age, confident that, in the providence of "our Father in heaven", even the corruption the Mishnah has sadly to recall is a sign that the Messiah is surely coming.

Finally, modern scholars often assert that, although some "Judaisms" had a Davidic Messiah, there were other "Judaisms" that looked for God alone to save his people at the End. This, too, is based on a misreading of the texts.

For example, there are very clear references to the Davidic Messiah in the *Psalms of Solomon* 17 and 18 yet these Psalms also insist that the Lord is King. Psalm 17 begins, "Lord, you are our King for ever and ever", and the same refrain occurs in verses 3, 34 and 46 (cf. *PsSol* 5.19). The Lord is said to be David's King (*PsSol* 17.34). Yet, in the same Psalm, David is called King (*PsSol* 17.4, 21, 32[twice], 42). Many messianic passages from the Bible are quoted or referred to, above all

---

[46] Danby (1933), p. 306, note 5; I am grateful to Dr Sacha Stern for pointing this out to me.
[47] Neusner (1984), p. 29.

2 Sam 7, Ps 89 and Isa 11. No Jew would have thought that the assertion that the Lord is King and the assertion that the Davidic Messiah is to be King were in competition; they would never have dreamed that one excluded the other, for was not the coming Davidic Messiah the totally obedient and just and holy anointed of the Lord? Two thrones, one rule.

T.W. Manson and Morton Smith argued that the expectation of a Davidic Messiah is entirely absent from the *Assumption of Moses* (*Testament of Moses*): "it is noteworthy that there is no Messiah: first comes the messenger and after him God himself and 'alone' (x.7 summus deus aeternus solus)."[48] When we turn to the passage about the messenger (nuntius), we find to our astonishment that this messenger, who is appointed chief (qui est in summo constitutus), is consecrated (a term used of the consecration of priests, but which must here refer to the consecration of a warrior)[49] and does exactly what God alone is to do in *AssMos* 10.7, avenge Israel and destroy her enemies. Charles sees that his literal reading of *AssMos* 10.7 leads to an inconsistency, and consequently he regards 10.1-2 as an insertion.[50] Tromp, rightly, notes that such duplication is not exceptional (Wisd 3.8; *1 Enoch* 91.12-14).[51] In *4 Ezra* 6.6 the Lord says that the End will come through Him and not through another, but this by no means excludes the statement in the same book that the End will come when all the nations gather to fight against the Son of God who will take his stand on Mount Zion and will destroy them (*4 Ezra* 13.32-38).

Finally, the canonical Psalms contain both Psalms about the enthronement of Yahweh and Psalms about the enthronement of the Davidic King. No one, except a modern commentator, would have thought that the enthronement of Yahweh excluded the enthronement of the Davidic King. Not only do the two types sit happily together in the canonical collection; there are even single Psalms, most clearly Psalm 89, which speak of the two: the psalmist refers to Yahweh as enthroned ("Justice and judgment are the habitation of thy throne" Ps 89.14) in a Psalm that recalls God's promise in 2 Sam 7 to build up the throne of David (Ps 89.4, 29, 36-37, 44).[52]

---

[48] Manson (1953), p. 32.
[49] Charles (1913), p. 421, note on *AssMos* 10.2.
[50] Charles (1913), p. 421, on 10.2.
[51] Trompf (1993), p. 231.
[52] O'Neill (1995), pp. 111-13.

Alleged non-Davidic Messiahs

Another of the ploys used by scholars to deny this steady central expectation of all who worshipped God in Israel is to point to the fact that Simon Bar Kosiba and many messianic pretenders mentioned by Josephus were not of Davidic descent. Even though most of these men acted like kings and like prophets, the lack of explicit reference to their davidic descent is supposed to show that non-davidic saving figures at the End were also expected. These scholars forget that any man could be descended from David through the female line. No one would have been ruled out as a possible Davidic Messiah if he could not claim to be descended from David through the patriarchal line, though obviously such descent would count mightily in favour. Josephus boasted that on his mother's side he was of royal descent (Josephus *Life* 2). The *Testament of Simeon* speaks of one person, "this one", whom the Lord will raise up from the tribe of Levi as High Priest and from the tribe of Judah as King (*TSim* 7.2).[53]

The Messiah would at first be hidden

The scholars who have denied that in Judaism there was a steady basic hope for the gathering in of the dispersion, for the rebuilding of Jerusalem and the Temple and for the reign of the son of David over a righteous kingdom to which all the Gentiles would come and submit have gone astray principally because they have not grasped one very important feature of the story. They have noticed that none of Josephus's messianic pretenders called himself explicitly the Davidic Messiah. That has led them to suppose that these men thought of themselves differently. The truth is that the silence of these men about who they thought they were is a part of the David story. We have abundance of evidence that all the figures in the End drama were to be unknown to their contemporaries. Anyone who read the Bible and awaited the End was free to ask whether one of their contemporaries was Elijah, or the Messiah, and none of these figures was permitted to say who they were. They had to be judged by what they otherwise did and said. The possibilities of mistake were endless. Any of the possible candidates could be simply a good man, or a bad man; he could be Elijah or he could be a false prophet; he could be the Messiah the son of David or he could be the Antichrist.

---

[53] See Hollander and de Jonge (1985), p. 126, note to *TSim* 7.2.

There are four arguments to support this case. First, the theme of secrecy and recognition is a basic theme of all prophecy; prophets faced both spiritual discernment and spiritual blindness and deafness. Secondly, there were clear indications in scripture that the Messiah would at first be hidden. Thirdly, the Messiah would have followers whose faithfulness would be tried and who would have to wait for vindication, and other people had to ask themselves whether or not they too should follow. Fourthly, the Messiah would be shadowed by an Antichrist, and the two contenders would have to fight it out in a battle the outcome of which would not at first be obvious.

First, the worshipper who read about how Jacob prophesied a surprising destiny for Judah, or Balaam the unlikely rising of a star out of Jacob and a sceptre out of Israel, or Nathan the unlikely reign of a son of David for ever would expect God to give sufficient clues to his purposes but would not expect those purposes to be obvious or likely. Samuel did not anoint any of the obvious elder sons of Jesse but surprisingly insisted that the youngest son, David, be called in from shepherding the sheep. The prophets, like Isaiah, were insisting that their vocation seemed almost to make the people's heart fat and their ears heavy and to shut their eyes (Isa 6.10). Therefore the worshippers had constantly to be attentive to the hidden revelations. If the Messiah were to come, they would expect there to be the need to discern who he was before the Lord made it obvious in the judgment of history.

Secondly, there were scriptural passages that assumed that the Messiah would be at first hidden, and these passages are echoed in other later Jewish writings of the late Second Temple or soon after. The Messiah would be born in Bethlehem, which implies a childhood and youth before his mission could be accomplished (Micah 5.1 (2); confirmed by the Targum).[54] Isa 7.1-14 foretelling the birth of a son from a virgin, whose name would be Emmanuel was also at least the promise of a child who was to grow up to be someone important. This passage is taken as messianic in *TJos* 19.3-5.[55]

Similarly, Isa 52.13-15 speaks of some one whose face was marred so that many "turned in horror from you"; kings in the future had to see something not told to them and understand something never heard. The Targum takes the servant who shall prosper and be exalted and great and very powerful of Isa 52.13 and names him the Messiah. Then it transfers all the talk of the marred visage to Israel itself. However, it does not remove the idea that Israel looked for the Messiah for

---

[54] See Vermes's important note, New Schürer (1979), vol. 2, pp. 523-25.
[55] O'Neill (1979).

many days. Even this seems to imply a hidden Messiah, looked for, and about to appear to vindicate his people. Zech 12, in a messianic passage in which God promises to pour upon the house of David the spirit of grace and of supplications, says, "they shall look upon me whom they have pierced, and they shall mourn for him, as one mourneth for an only son" (Zech 12.10); then follows a day when there shall be a fountain opened to the house of David for sin and for uncleanness (Zech 13.1).

Outside the Bible there are clear references to the hidden Messiah. *Ethiopic Enoch* (*1 Enoch*) 62.1 says, "Open your eyes and lift up your horns if ye are able to recognize the Elect One." Wisdom of Solomon 5 begins, "Then the righteous man will stand with great confidence in the presence of those who have afflicted him, and those who make light of his labours." In *4 Ezra* the Lord says to the nations, "Look now, and understand whom you have denied, whom you have not served, whose commandments you have despised." (*4 Ezra* 7.37).[56]

The history of David was full of hiddenness. There is the curious incident at the slaying of Goliath when Saul does not recognise David (1 Sam 17.55-58), a fact played upon in Pseudo-Philo *Biblical Antiquities* 61.9; cf. 18.11. Although David has been anointed by Samuel, he has to fight for his throne against Saul. Even on his throne he is expelled from Jerusalem by his son Absalom and has to hide. In Psalm 27, a Psalm of David, the psalmist says that in the time of trouble the Lord will hide him in the secret of his tabernacle before setting him up on a rock (Ps 27.5), implying that only a faithful observer, who knew God's hidden plans, would have recognized him for what he was. The whole history of David is a history of an embattled king who is despised and who has to hide before resuming his proper glory. The coming Messiah could well have been thought of in similar terms.

Thirdly, the Messiah will have followers whose true glory will not at first be obvious. In *4 Ezra* 13.51 the Lord says to Ezra in explanation of his vision of a man coming up out of the sea, "Just as no one can explore or know what is in the depths of the sea, so no one on earth can see my Son or those who are with him, except in the time of his day." If the words "or those who are with him" had not been there, we could have thought that this was just one of those passages that spoke of a sudden coming of the Messiah who was waiting in heaven. The references to the companions of the Messiah puts another complexion of things. If the Son has companions, this implies a hidden

---

[56] Cf. Barker (1996), p.19, note 30.

ministry when disciples gathered around him. The hiddenness of the Son with his companions implies that the prophet had both taught and gathered sons of the prophet before the prophet's true status was disclosed. Similarly the Son of Man is hidden and revealed to the elect before he is disclosed to his enemies, the kings and the mighty rulers of the earth in *1 Enoch* 62.6-16. The "sowing" of the elect before the day of vengeance (*1 Enoch* 62.8) implies a hidden activity of the Son of Man on earth, during which he gathers the elect, before the disclosure of his glory.

This explains why non-committed bystanders could speculate about a prophet as to whether or not he was the Messiah. Wisdom of Solomon 2.16-20 records the musings of hostile observers: "Let us see if his words are true, and let us test what will happen at the end of his life; for if the righteous man is God's Son, he will help him... Let us test him with insult and torture..." This almost certainly refers to the Messiah, but even if it doesn't, it still shows that the truly righteous are not obvious and there are tests that could be performed to see if anyone is really favoured by God. I have deliberately not brought the New Testament evidence into play, but surely here it can be allowed that the numerous occasions in which John the Baptist and Jesus are examined as to whether or not either of them is the Messiah are likely to be authentic. People adduce certain facts as counting against Jesus' being the Messiah, for example: that he comes from Galilee or from Nazareth and not from Bethlehem (John 1.46; 7.41,42,52), that he is a Samaritan or illegitimate (John 8.41, 48); they wonder whether he is Elijah or one of the prophets (Matt 14.1-2; Mark 6.14-16; Luke 9.7-9; Matt 16.14; Mark 8.28; Luke 9.19). The central argument of Gamaliel's speech is no doubt put in a more favourable light in Acts than in the original, but there does not seem to be any reason to doubt that a Rabbi could advise his hearers to let a messianic movement alone on the grounds that God would eventually show whether or not it was bogus. But this implies that the Messiah could be hidden for a time (Acts 5.33-39).

Fourthly, the Messiah was to be shadowed by an Antichrist. In the end it would come to a battle in which the Antichrist would be conquered by the Messiah. This implies a battle for people's allegiance as well as, later, a battle for mastery. Satan was envisaged as having an agent on earth who would try to deceive people into thinking that he was the Messiah. The idea is clearly found in the Bible, particularly in Nahum 1. Beliar is overthrown by the messenger of good tidings whose feet are on the mountains (Nah 2.1; English 1.15). In *TLevi* 18, the Star of Num 24 who will arise as a King will eventually bind Beliar and power will be given to the Messiah's sons to tread on the evil spirits who are Beliar's servants (*TLevi* 18.12). In *2 Bar* 39.7-40.4 the Anointed One is revealed to be like the vine and the fountain in the parable, and he binds the last ruler. The Qumran sectaries had watched a struggle between the Teacher of Righteousness and the Man of Lies which had temporarily ended in the death of the Teacher; but the Teacher is to come again as the Messiah of Aaron and of Israel. I think they believed the Teacher to be the Messiah, but, leaving that aside, it is clear that the Man of Lies represents the power of evil that is destined to be destroyed at the End (CD 1.14; 8.13; 20.15; 1QpHab 2.1; 5.11). There is a terrible curse on someone who has betrayed the community. He is called Melchi-Resha', which means King of Wickedness, the opposite of Melchizedek, King of Righteousness (4Q280). An additional Psalm at Qumran calls on Judah to rejoice because in Judah is no Beliar (4Q88 10.7-8,10). The battle between the Sons of Light and the Sons of Darkness in 1QM, the War Scroll, implies that there are on earth agents of God and of Satan; I think that the general opinion that there is no Messiah in 1QM has ignored the meaning of the references to the King of Glory, the Valiant One, the glorious Man who fights at the head of the righteous army (1QM 12.8, 10-12).[57]

The characteristic feature of the Man of Lawlessness, the Son of Perdition, is that he deceives the people with every miracle and with signs and with marvels of deception (2 Thess 2.9; *SibOr* 3.66-67). He could not deceive if the contest between him and the Messiah was open and settled. Presumably the claims by Jesus' opponents that he was casting out devils in the power of the Devil were a charge that he was not the Christ but the Antichrist.

All four arguments: from the general nature of prophecy that discernment was always necessary right up to the End, from the explicit references in the Bible to the hiddenness of the Messiah, from the assumption that the Messiah would already have followers before he was revealed in glory, and from the fact that the battle between Christ and the Antichrist is assumed to rage on earth before the End we can conclude that the belief that the Messiah the son of David would be hidden and hard to recognize was a settled part of Jewish messianism.

---

[57] O'Neill (1995), pp. 72-73.

What would the Messiah be like?

This conclusion has momentous consequences. If spiritual discernment was always required of Israel, how much more was it required in the days when the Messiah was growing up among them and beginning to carry out his task of unmasking the forces of evil and battling against them in order to liberate Jerusalem so that the people would gather again and the nations would flock to worship?

They were looking for one Messiah, the son of David. The scholars who resist this case have tried to show that there were Jews who expected non-Davidic Messiahs. Most of these, like the Messiah of Israel or the Messiah of Judah or the Prince of the Congregation or the supposed King of Egypt of *SibOr* 3.286-294[58] are simply examples of a failure to recognise clear references to the three key messianic texts in Gen 49, Num 24 and 2 Sam 7 and their echoes in the rest of the Bible. Great play has been made of the supposed belief, represented in the Qumran writings and the *Testaments of the Twelve Patriarchs*, that two Messiahs would come, the Messiah of Aaron and the Messiah of Judah, the Priestly Messiah and the Kingly Messiah. It has also been argued that a Messiah of Joseph would come before the Messiah of David as a separate, suffering figure.[59] These two theories, however, do little to support the idea of a non-Davidic messiahship for they often appear together with the Messiah of David.

I wish to argue that the Qumran view of the Messiah and the traditions that call on the figure of Joseph are both examples of a more general tendency to look in the Bible for other clues as to what the one Davidic Messiah would be like. The Bible provided both types and antitypes of the one Messiah.

Let us begin with the alleged two Messiahs of Qumran and the *Testaments of the Twelve Patriarchs*. First, there is only a single passage in the Dead Sea Scrolls where the word *Messiah* referring to the one of Aaron and Israel occurs in the plural, the passage about the steadfastness of the men of holiness in the Manual of Discipline: "they shall be ruled by the first ordinances in which the members of the community began their instruction [a reference to the foundation teaching of the Teacher of Righteousness] until the coming of the Prophet and the Anointed Ones of Aaron and Israel [to follow the normal interpretation]" (1QS 9.10-11). All other references to the Messiah of Aaron and Israel are in the singular: one Messiah of two tribes. It is more

---

[58] Pomykala (1995), pp. 23-264.
[59] Dalman (1888); O'Neill (1994b), p. 196 note 24, for bibliography.

likely that this plural is a plural of majesty than that we should emend all the other references, in the Damascus Document found in the Cairo Geniza at the end of the last century as well as in the scrolls found at Qumran. In fact, all three titles (Prophet, Messiah of Aaron, Messiah of Israel) should probably be referred to the one figure who is a Prophet like Moses, anointed as Priest, and anointed as King.[60] Similarly, there is no clear separation of two Messiahs in the *Testaments of the Twelve Patriarchs*: the Messiah son of Levi is also King (*TLevi* 18.3) and, although the Messiah of Judah can be spoken of alone (*TJudah* 24), the Messiah of Levi is never spoken of except as also Messiah of Judah.[61]

The Messiah of Joseph is also referred to in the *Testaments of the Twelve Patriarchs* when Jacob his father blesses him for his willingness to suffer in order to save his brothers and their father from famine and sees in him a type of the "prophecy of heaven concerning the Lamb of God and Saviour of the world, because as spotless he will be given up for lawless men, and as sinless he will die for the unfaithful in the blood of the covenant for the salvation of the Gentiles and Israel, and he will destroy Beliar and those who serve him" (*TBen* 3.8). This can hardly be a Christian interpolation into the Testaments, for no Christian scribe, being a believer in the Virgin Birth, would invent a messianic prophecy about a son of Joseph.[62] The figure of Joseph as an innocent sufferer for the good of Israel is taken as giving a clue to what the Messiah of David would be like.

Similarly, the long romance of Joseph and Asenath takes Joseph as the Son of God who redeems Asenath, the abandoned daughter of Dinah who has been adopted (according to Jewish legend) by Potiphar the priest of On, and she stands for apostate Israel.[63] A fragmentary *Joseph Apocryphon* from Cave 4 at Qumran contains a prayer of Joseph, "My Father and my God, do not abandon me to the hand of the Gentiles. Execute in [by?] me judgment (*'sh 'th by mšpt*) so that the afflicted and the poor may not perish" (4Q371 1.16-17). Note that the speaker in the Hymn Scroll similarly says that "in *or* by me you [God] have distinguished between just and guilty" (1QH 7.12; 4.8, 27). Joseph in the fragment extols the absolute power of God who will subdue all the

---

[60] O'Neill (1995), pp. 39-40. *Messiahs* in the plural refers to anointed prophets in 1QM 11.7; 4Q270 2 2.14.
[61] De Jonge (1986); O'Neill (1979).
[62] O'Neill (1979), pp. 7-9.
[63] O'Neill (1994b).

Gentiles who hold them captive (4Q372).[64] The deliverance of the afflicted and the poor and the subduing of the Gentiles is the work of the Davidic Messiah.

My thesis is beautifully illustrated by the case of Melchizedek. Melchizedek is already related to David in the Bible in Psalm 110 in which the historic David's Lord is addressed by Yahweh and enthroned as priest for ever after the order of Melchizedek. In the Qumran Melchizedek fragment, Melchizedek is the Judge in one of the Songs of David (Ps 82); he is seen as the *messenger* of Isa 52.7; he is called *The Messiah of the Spirit* and identified with the *Prince* of Dan 9.25 and the *comforter* of Isa 61.2-3 (11QMelch). The use of the Psalm 82 links this figure with David and it is surely implied that this heavenly Melchizedek is the one referred to as David's Lord in Psalm 110.

The messianic significance of Isaac has recently been strongly denied by Alan Segal. He argues that all the Jewish evidence of the first century on Binding of Isaac "was used especially to clarify the meaning of martyrdom and encourage Jews in persecution." The most important point is that "the story is nowhere used as a prototype of messianic suffering."[65]

Segal brackets out the evidence of the Targums on the grounds that, although we know that targums were used in the first century, we have no way of isolating the first century traditions contained in them.[66] I am reluctant to believe that the targumists, much later on, deliberately made up interpretations of the Binding of Isaac that brought the story closer to the Christian use of the passage as a type of the suffering Messiah who gave himself as a sacrifice for sin.[67] The Fragmentary Targum records the prayer of Abraham, "Now...when the children of Isaac come to a time of distress, you may remember on their behalf the binding of Isaac their father, and loose and forgive them their sins and deliver them from all distress..."[68] But, leaving the Targum to one side, Segal's case is not watertight.

Segal concedes that the Bible itself identifies Mount Moriah with Mount Zion (2 Chron 3.1), and that *Jubilees* 17.15–18.19 dates the Binding of Isaac at Passover. He rather underplays the connection of Isaac's binding and the vicarious martyrdoms reported in *4 Maccabees*. Eleazar, who prays at his martyrdom that God would take his blood as

---

[64] Schuller (1990).
[65] Segal (1996), p. 108.
[66] Segal (1996), p. 106.
[67] O'Neill (1981), pp. 13-15; Horbury (1981), pp. 169-71.
[68] Vermes (1961).

the people's purification and his life as an exchange for theirs (*4 Macc* 6.27-30) is specifically said, in chapter 7, to exercise reason like that of Isaac in rendering the many-headed rack ineffective (*4 Macc* 7.14). But elsewhere, in telling the story of the martyrdom of the seven brothers who are encouraged in their steadfastness by their mother, the example of Abraham and Isaac is frequently invoked. The brothers encourage each other by recalling Abraham by whose hand Isaac would have submitted to being slain, and by reminding themselves that if they die faithfully, Abraham and Isaac and Jacob would welcome them, and all the fathers would praise them (*4 Macc* 13.12, 17). This must refer to the general resurrection and so to the day of the Messiah (Ezek 37.24). The mother is compare to Abraham (*4 Macc* 15.28; 17.6; 18.20); and she reminds her sons that their father used to teach them of Isaac who was offered as a burnt-offering (*4 Macc* 18.11). Above all, she calls on her sons to offer themselves in sacrifice like Isaac (*4 Macc* 16.19-20). It seems artificial to separate the story of the seven brothers, as only an example of martyrdom, from the prayer of Eleazar, which regards his death as also vicarious; and it seems artificial to deny to Isaac's Binding vicarious power since Isaac is mentioned prominently in the story of the death of the seven brothers and Isaac is linked distinctly to Eleazar's death.

Finally, Segal has overlooked two other early passages that give sacrificial power to the Binding of Isaac. In Pseudo-Philo's *Biblical Antiquities* it is recounted that God required Abraham's son Isaac as a burnt offering. God is speaking. "[Abraham] brought him that he should be prepared as a sacrifice on the altar, but I returned him to his father and, because he did not resist, his oblation was made acceptable in my sight and because of his blood I have chosen this people" (18.5). The second passage is from the Hymn Scroll at Qumran. The speaker of the hymn, probably rightly identified with the Teacher of Righteousness, says in addressing God, "My father knew me not and my mother abandoned me to Thee", a possible reference to Abraham and Isaac and Hannah and Samuel (1QH 9.35). The speaker of the Hymn Scroll is the source of living waters (1QH 8.4, 16, 21; 18.10, 12) who through suffering attains a crown (1QH 9.23-26). If the community as a whole by suffering was to offer expiation for the land (1QS 8.4-10; 1QSa 1.3), surely their leader must also have been thought to suffer for the land. In the fourth cave there has turned up an Aramaic fragment that says just this: "He will make atonement for all the children of his generation…His word shall be as the word of heaven and his teaching shall be according to the will of God. His eternal sun shall burn brilliantly. The fire shall be kindled in all the corners of the earth... They will speak many words against him. There will be many lies... He will overthrow his evil generation... When he arises there will be lying and violence..." (4Q451 9.1-6). This language echoes the Biblical language about the coming King, like a burning sun, who will be opposed by lies.

It seems that the Binding of Isaac was actually linked to Passover, the season when, according to old tradition, the Messiah was to come (Jer 38 (31).8 LXX).[69] The Binding, although not an actual sacrifice, was treated as such. It was linked to the martyr sacrifice of Eleazar that was regarded as sacrificial and atoning.

There is one feature of the original story of the Binding of Isaac in Gen 22 that lends support to the case I am making. Abraham at the end calls the mount, The Lord sees, and it is said that to this day, "In the mount of the Lord it shall be seen." The LXX interprets this obscure sentence to mean, "In the mount the Lord is seen" (Gen 22.14). As the mount is Mount Zion, the obscure popular saying could refer both to the coming of the Lord God to redeem his people and to the coming of his Messiah.

The fleeting references to the Binding of Isaac in the New Testament seem (*pace* Segal) to reflect a given theology that was already current in Judaism rather than an entirely new connection of ideas first made by followers of Jesus of Nazareth (John 3.16; Rom 8.32; Heb 11.17-19).

Moses is specifically told a Prophet like him will arise (Deut 18.18-19). This is taken to be messianic in the New Testament in John 6.14; Acts 3.22 and 7.37, but was it messianic in the other Jewish sources of our period? The passage is reproduced in the striking collection of testimonies discovered in the fourth cave at Qumran (4QTest = 4Q175 lines 5-8). Each of the testimonies is marked by a blank at the end of the last line of each section, and the beginning of the next testimony is marked in the margin by a sign in the shape of a hook.[70] The first testimony consists of verses from Deut 5 and the prophecy of the prophet from Deut 18. The second quotes part of Balaam's prophecy about the star from Jacob and the sceptre out of Israel (Num 24.15-17). The third quotes Moses' blessing on Levi from Deut 33.8-11. The fourth is a prophecy of Joshua made up of Joshua 6.26 and an unknown Psalm of Joshua cursing a cursed agent of Belial and his two sons. In the light of the interpretation of 1QS 9.11 given above, it would seem to be

---

[69] O'Neill (1995), p. 117 and note 7.
[70] Dupont-Sommer (1961), p. 315.

right to read this as a prophecy, drawn from the Bible, of a Messiah who would be Prophet, King and Priest.

In the drama *The Exodus* by Ezekiel the Tragedian preserved by Eusebius Moses recounts to his father-in-law a dream in which he saw on the summit of a mountain a great throne that extended to heaven on which sat a noble man wearing a crown and holding a sceptre in his left hand. He gave the sceptre to Moses and told him to sit on the great throne and gave him his crown and withdrew. Moses saw the earth, what was beneath the earth and above the heavens, the stars fell on their knees before him, and he numbered them all (verses 68-82). Moses was afraid and awoke. His father-in-law interpreted the dream as favourable: Moses would erect a great throne and would adjudicate and lead mortals; he would see things present, past and future (verses 83-89). Holladay rightly points out that God reminds Moses later in the drama that he is mortal (verse 101). I would interpret the dream as an example of how Moses himself is used as a type of the heavenly Son of Man; Moses in his dream sees himself put in the place of the heavenly Man, meaning that anyone who wants to know more about the Man should look at Moses, specifically at his wisdom in numbering the stars, at his law-giving and teaching, and at his prophetic power.

Joshua is already seen as messianic because the story of his making the sun stand still is one of the three texts said by Josephus to be specifically stored in the Temple; the other two are the Song of Moses, Deut 32, and the song of the well, Num 21.17-20 which is an important prophecy used in the Damascus Document to portray the role of the Seeker of the Law who will come as the Teacher of Righteousness at the end of the days (Josephus *Ant* 3.38; 4.303; 5.61; cf. CD 6.2-11).

In the *Sibylline Oracles* there is a curious section that reads (translating the text and not adopting any of the usual conjectural emendations):

> A certain one will come again from heaven, the most eminent of men,
> To where he spread upon the fruitful wood his hands—
> The best one of the Hebrews, who once made the sun stand still
> By crying with noble speech and lips unsullied. (*SibOr* 5.256-259)[71]

The best of the Hebrews, a tall man from heaven, returns to where he was crucified. He is like Joshua in that he made the sun stand still. The tall man in heaven is the Son of God (*5 Ezra* 2.43, 47: a young man of great stature, taller than any of the others;[72] *Shepherd of Hermas* Sim

---

[71] O'Neill (1991a), p. 91
[72] *5 Ezra* is a Jewish text and not, as often assumed, Christian; O'Neill (1991b).

9.6.1). So the Messiah is seen as foreshadowed by Joshua, particularly as he caused the sun to stand still while he conquered the enemy. The figure at Dura Europos with the sun, moon and seven stars at his head is perhaps meant to represent Joshua: he said, "Sun, stand thou still upon Gibeon; and thou, Moon, in the valley of Ajalon... So the sun stood still in the midst of heaven, and hasted not to go down about a whole day"; the Lord hearkened unto the voice of a man (Josh 10.12-14).

So not only the stories of David, but also the stories of Melchizedek and Isaac and Joseph and Levi and Moses and Aaron and Joshua could be drawn upon for information about what the Messiah would be like.

There is a negative example, Josephus's application of a messianic prophecy to Vespasian. The historian Josephus ascribed the disastrous Jewish War "above all to an ambiguous oracle ... found in their sacred scriptures that at that time there would be someone from their land who would rule the world." This is probably a reference to Gen 49.10 or to Balaam's prophecy in Num 24 (Num 24.7-9; 17-19). Many of the wise thought it referred to someone of their own nation, but Josephus argues that it really referred to Vespasian who was proclaimed emperor on Jewish soil (Josephus *War* 6.310-315). Josephus made his fortune by privately prophesying to Vespasian that Nero's successors would not long reign and that Vespasian would be Caesar and his son would be Caesar (Josephus *War* 3.399-408). This prophecy is independently reported by Tacitus (*History* 5.13) and by Suetonius (*Vespasian* 4).

Josephus, then, confirms the thesis I have been arguing. The Jewish revolt was largely fuelled by men who believed that the messianic prophecies in Gen 49 and Num 24 applied to them, and that they were destined, after an armed struggle, to rule the world as God's Messiah. Josephus does not deny that these prophecies in the Bible are inspired, but he interpreted them in a non-messianic sense as applying to the Roman empire. He had some basis for this in the reference at the end of Balaam's prophecy to the ships from the coast of the Kittim who would afflict Ashur and Eber (Num 24.24). The Qumran sectaries identified the Kittim of Assur as the Romans who had conquered Syria and who were, according to Dan 11.30-32, supporters of the wicked of the covenant (1QM 1.1-14 *et passim*). Josephus took the opposite line. Josephus also had a messianic expectation beyond even the great Roman empire, but his reading of the stone passage in Dan 2.44-45 he preferred not to commit to writing; this stone would destroy the kingdom of iron, brass, clay, silver and gold, the Roman empire and all other possible empires (Josephus *Ant* 10.210). Josephus can hardly have renounced the hope for a Davidic Messiah, for he records David's dying charge to Solomon that, if Solomon kept Moses' commandments, the kingdom would be secured to their line and "no other house should rule over the Hebrews than ours for every age" (Josephus *Ant* 7.385). Of course the succession of David did end (Josephus *Ant* 10.143 etc.), but the tradition is there that, if Israel kept the law of Moses, the Davidic house would throw up the Stone who would rule all nations. Josephus did not want his fellow Jews to think that this was imminent, but he did not renounce the ultimate hope.

Not only were people in the Bible types of the Messiah, but the Messiah was held to have been spoken about in the Bible as present in the history of humanity and of Israel.

The Image of God and The Rock

The Messiah was also seen in the Bible by signs of his actual presence in the Biblical narrative of salvation. He was thought of as The Image of God according to which Adam is made; and Adam as the antitype. At the end "the Last One arrives and he will bring out Adam and the Fathers and lead them into Eden so that they may be filled with joy" (*2 En* 42.5J). The term *Son of Man* indicates that the conquering figure who is to be enthroned is the anti-type of Adam, Son of Adam.

Are there any traces in Jewish writings of the time of such a settled reading of Gen 1.26-27 according to which God always had with him a being that was named *The Image of God*? Are there any traces in Jewish writings of the time that such a being could have been thought of as coming down from heaven and living as a man on earth?

Philo of Alexandria has preserved many traditions, not all of which fit neatly into one system. Among those traditions there is abundant evidence for the exegesis of Gen 1.27 that we can deduce from the scattered New Testament passages.

In *de somniis* i.239 Philo gives a tradition that says that, just as those who cannot see the sun itself see the rays of the sun, and just as they see the halo around the moon as the moon itself, so they comprehend the Image of God, the Word his messenger, as God himself. Similarly in *de confusione linguarum* 97, those who choose Moses to be their guide, and see (Ex 24.10), desire to see God; if they cannot see God, they see his Image, the most holy Word.

In a complicated set of traditions in *de fuga et inventione* 100-101, the words of Ex 25.21, "I will speak to you above the mercy-seat, between the two cherubim," are interpreted allegorically. The two cherubim are the two Powers of God, the Creative Power and the Royal Power. He who speaks from above the mercy-seat is the divine Word which is invisible yet is called The Image of God, the most ancient of the objects of the intellect, the one who is nearest to the Only One. Finally, the Word is the Charioteer of the Powers.

In *de confusione linguarum* 146 anyone who is not yet worthy of being called one of the sons of God should labour earnestly to be adorned according to his Firstborn, the Word, the eldest of the angels, as it were Archangel, bearing many names, for he is Beginning and Name of God and Word. (I think we should stop here, because the next tradition describes not the Word but the faithful seeker, who is to be named The man according to the Image, the One who Sees, Israel.)

This Word is said, in another tradition reported by Philo, to be the Image of God through whom the world was all at once made *(de specialibus legibus* i.81). In *legum allegoriarum* iii.95-96 Philo reproduces an ancient tradition about the meaning of the name Bezaleel (Ex 21.2). It means In the shadow of God. The Shadow of God is his Word by which, as with an instrument, he made the world. This Shadow or Model is the archetype of others. As God is the paradigm of the Image (which is now called Shadow), so the Image becomes the paradigm of others. As the beginning of Genesis says, And God made man according to the Image of God.

The idea that the Word was the agent of creation is, of course, found in Wisdom 9.1 and many other places, but can we find in Jewish writings any inkling of the notion that the Word or the Image of God might be born as a man and live in this world? In *de agricultura* 51, Exod 23.20, I will send my messenger before your face, is interpreted of the Right Word and the Firstborn Son. In *de praemiis et poenis* 95, the important messianic prophecy of Balaam in Num 24.7 is referred to in the following words: There will come forth a Man, says the oracle, and leading his host and fighting he will subdue great and populous nations (Num 24.17 cf. LXX). This corresponds to the tradition in Wisd 18.15-16 which tells of the all-powerful Word leaping from heaven out of the royal thrones, a stern warrior in the midst of the doomed land bearing as a sharp sword God's unfeigned commandment, filling all things with death. This Word touches heaven while treading on earth: a tall one, like the Son of God in *5 Ezra* 2.43 and the Best of the Hebrews in *SibOr* 5.256-259.

Another hidden sign of the presence of Christ in the Bible is given in the presence of the Stone.

There is a rabbinic tradition that the rock that Moses struck (Ex 17.6) followed around the wilderness generation and stationed itself before the tabernacle at each stopping place (cf. *Moh. Sura* 7.11d).[73] In 1 Cor 10.4 the Rock of Moses that he strikes to give the people water is Christ, and the very casualness of the reference is a sign that this an ancient and current traditional interpretation of the wilderness wanderings. (Compare the statement in Heb 11.25-26 that Moses preferred to suffer with his people rather than enjoy the pleasures of sin and esteemed the reproach of Christ greater riches than the treasures in Egypt; *the reproach of Christ* is equated with the suffering of the people both in Egypt and in their desert wanderings.) But that rock seems to be the same rock that appears in many other places in the Bible and in tradition.

Let us begin with the rock at Bethel. Bethel was taken to be the site of the Temple in Jerusalem in the Targums, a tradition confirmed by 11QTemple Scroll 29.8-10:

> I will dwell with them for ever and ever and will sanctify my sanctuary by my glory. I will cause my glory to rest on it until the day of creation on which I shall create my sanctuary, establishing it for myself for all time according to the covenant which I have made with Jacob in Bethel (cf. *TLevi* 9.3).

Joachim Jeremias drew attention to the rabbinic tradition that the stone at Bethel was the holy stone that God made before he made the world; on the basis of this stone he spread out the world. (*Yalqut Gen* 120 (on Gen 28.22); *Pirqe Rabbi Eliezer* 32; 35; *Zohar Gen* on Gen 28.22).[74] According to Gen 28.17, 22 the stone at Bethel was also the place of the presence of God: the house of God (*Zohar Gen* on Gen 28.22 ed. Romm, Wilna, 1894, p. 231); it was also the door of heaven (Gen 28.17; Ps Jon Gen 28.11).

The stone at Bethel is the stone of the altar at Jerusalem. That same stone was probably also identified with the altar which Abraham built on Mount Moriah, for Mount Moriah was the site of the House of the Lord that Solomon built (2 Chron 3.1): "and Abraham built an altar there, and laid the wood in order, and bound Isaac his son, and laid him on the altar upon the wood" (Gen 22.9). The Targum Pseudo-Jonathan reads, "And Abraham built the altar there which Adam built,

---

[73] Gutmann (1992), p. 141.
[74] Jeremias (1928); cf. W. Traub, (1954), p. 530; English, p. 530: "als Messias is Jesus 'Bethel' die Stätte Gottes, die Pforte des Himmels auf Erden"; see also Jeremias (1926), pp. 51-58 at p. 53.

which had been destroyed by the waters of the flood, and which Noah had rebuilt." So the stone on which the Lord spread out the world was the stone that Adam built as an altar (where Abel and Cain offered their respective sacrifices), that Noah rebuilt (Gen 8.20), that Abraham built into an altar on which to offer Isaac, that Solomon had built into the Temple at Jerusalem.

Jeremias concluded that in John 1.51 Jesus identified himself with the stone: where he was, the presence of God was; where he was, there was the gate of heaven; where he was, there the spirits of God were standing ready to serve and to bring the bread of life, the living word of God, down to earth.

It is unlikely that this son of man saying is a self reference since it clearly speaks about a supernatural figure. Nevertheless, Jeremias has rightly noticed that the Son of Man is a title given to the stone anointed by Jacob (Gen 28.18). Justin Martyr drew attention to the tradition that a messianic significance was attached to the anointing of the stone by Jacob in Gen 28: "And that the stone is Christ is proclaimed symbolically by many passages of scripture as we have likewise shown" (*Dial* 86; cf. 58; 126). Philo cites some persons who took the word *place* in Gen 28.2 *he lighted upon a certain place* as referring to the divine Logos (*de somniis* 1.118), and this might refer to the stone that was lying there in that place, upon which Jacob had his dream, and which was later set up as altar. Ken Howcroft drew my attention to *de migratione Abrahami* 5-6: where the house of God of Gen 28.17 is identified with the Word by which the Ruler of the universe governs all things.

The identification of a stone with a person was made easier by the messianic interpretation of the stone in Dan 2 that crushed his enemies, human enemies who are also symbolised by the image of iron and clay or of iron, brass, clay silver and gold (Dan 2.34, 45; Josephus *Ant* 10.210). The Teacher of Righteousness seems to be compared to a foundation stone, and the sectaries were living stones made into a house (1QH 6.25-27; 7.4,8-9).

The angels at Bethel would then be seen as taking up the prayers of the people, symbolized by the smoke of sacrifice, from the altar into heaven, for the angels are commonly in Judaism the intercessors for Israel (*1 Enoch* 40; Tob 12.12; 11.14; 3.16; 12.15; *Jub* 30.20; *TDan* 6.2; *TAsh* 6.4-7; *TLevi* 5);[75] this tradition is vividly represented in Rev 8.4 etc. Origen records a Jewish tradition about angels.

---

[75] Bousset-Gressmann (1926), p. 330.

They ascend bringing the prayers of men into the purest heavenly region of the universe, or even to places purer than these beyond the heavens. And again they descend from there bringing to each individual according to his merits some benefit which God commands them to administer to those who are to receive his favours. (*cCelsum* 5.4, trans. H. Chadwick, p. 266)

So it seems that the Son of Man is both the stone on the basis of which the world was made and the altar stone at Bethel/Jerusalem from which the angels take the prayers of the people and to which they bring back the heavenly answers to those prayers.

All Jews thought that the davidic Messiah would suffer; some also thought that he would have to die.

This web of tradition has momentous consequences. If the Son of Man in John 1.52 is the place of sacrifice, presumably he is also the sacrificial victim, the High Priest who takes his own blood into the holy of holies (Heb 9.12; 10.19). The altar, of course, signifies what is sacrificed on it (Matt 23.18-20, a philological point as well as a moral point; cf. 1 Cor 9.13: "they which wait at the altar are partakers with the altar"; Heb 13.10: "we have an altar of which those who serve the tabernacle have no right to eat"). John 1.52 has preserved for us an ancient Jewish tradition that taught that the Son of Man would be seen as the altar and the sacrificial victim on the altar to which the people would come and, as participating in that sacrifice, see the angels taking their prayers to heaven and coming back with the gracious answers to their petitions. The symbol of this Son of Man was the stone at Bethel upon which Jacob had his dream and which he later set up and anointed; this altar was in the house of God, and was the gate of heaven.

The Davidic typology itself entailed the idea that the Messiah would have a humble and obscure birth and that he would have to suffer before he entered into his kingdom and that he would have to suffer even in his kingdom: in the Temple liturgy Psalm 132.1 would be sung as a Messianic prayer, "Lord, remember David, and all his afflictions."[76] The hiddenness of the Messiah was one more indication of the sin of the people. The Targum Pseudo-Jonathan of Micah 4.8 says, "And you, O Messiah of Israel, who have been hidden away from the sins of the congregation of Zion, the kingdom is destined to come to

---

[76] O'Neill (1995), p. 42.

you, and the former dominion shall be restored to the kingdom of the congregation of Jerusalem."[77]

The figure of Isaac on the altar was a poignant reminder of the sins of Israel and the love and mercy of God who was willing to remember Isaac on behalf of the people (Targums on Gen 22). It was also a type of the sufferings of the Messiah. The image of Isaac was used to supplement and enrich the image of the greater son of David. The prominent place given in the Song of the Four Nights to the offering of Isaac on the second night in parallel to the coming of Moses and the Messiah on the fourth Night at the End is no accident. In worship, the willingness of Isaac to offer himself at the hand of his father was taken as pointing to the willingness of the Son of God to offer himself at the hand of his Father.

This is not just a prejudiced Christian reading of Jewish tradition. The Qumran scrolls now reveal to us a movement in Judaism that looked back at a suffering and crucified Teacher of Righteousness who would come at the End as the Messiah of Aaron and of Israel.[78]

A controversy between Jesus and the scribes has sometimes been cited as showing that Jesus did not think the Messiah was to be David's son. Jesus quoted the opening words of Psalm 110 (Matt 22.41-45; Mark 12.35-37; Luke 20.41-44). He then said, "If therefore David calls him [the Messiah] Lord, how is [the Messiah] David's son?" (Matt 22.45). These words do not mean that one seated at the right hand is not the son of David. They mean that the one seated at the right hand is both son of David and David's Lord and, later in the same psalm, high priest after the order of Melchizedek. The son of David has enemies; he has been exalted far above them (although, by implication, he has suffered at their hands); and he reigns until all enemies are put under his feet.

Does the story of the encounter of two travellers with Jesus on Road to Emmaus (Luke 24, esp. 19-24; 25-27) contradict my assertion that everyone thought that the Messiah would have to suffer? Is the redemption of Israel ruled out if the potential redeemer suffers? I think not. Notice, first, that this is another example of people discussing whether or not this man or that man was the Messiah. Everyone could have expected that the Messiah would have to face some trials and tribulations before restoring the kingdom to Israel. His death would raise a sharp question; the Sadducees, who rejected the possibility of resurrection, would not have been able to accept a crucified redeemer.

---

[77] Levey (1974), p. 92.
[78] O'Neill (1995), chapter 4.

The empty tomb was already another piece of evidence to be weighed. The clear teaching, based on scripture, which Jesus was able to give, would show that not only sufferings, but death, were foretold; not only death, but also entry into glory.

Conclusion: Dura murals

It is remarkable how many of the images that we have been discussing are found in the murals at Dura Europos: not only David the shepherd king, chosen by Samuel above his brothers; not only David weeping and barefoot ascending Mount Olivet, head covered; not only David reuniting the twelve tribes after they have been raised from the valley of dry bones; but the Sacrifice of Isaac, Jacob's pillow, and the Rock of Moses. Perhaps Mordecai and Haman should be ranked here: Mordecai arrayed like a king mounted on a horse and Haman his enemy who had tried to destroy Israel, shortly to be raised on the gallows he had prepared for the righteous Jew.

What would the Messiah be like? He would be like King David, of course, for Jacob's Blessings in Gen 49, Balaam's prophecies in Num 24 and Nathan's pronouncement of the promises of God in 2 Sam 7 were constitutive of Israel's hope. But the David typology was supplemented by hints gathered from Adam, from Melchizedek, from Isaac, from Joseph and from Moses and Aaron. The Messiah had always been present and active in the history of the world. Man was made according to this Image and the stone upon which the world was created was Adam's altar, Noah's altar, Abraham's altar on Mt Moriah, the stone that was Jacob's pillow, and the altar stone of the Temple at Jerusalem. Jews at the time of Jesus had a fixed centre to their hopes for the Messiah: he would be the greater son of David. But there were other potent hints. They expected him to have to suffer like David. Some of them believed he had come and had been crucified on the Day of Atonement. Others believed he had been crucified at Passover when the lambs for the Passover sacrifice were being offered. His glory was hidden because of the sins of the people, but the time would come when that glory was revealed. Then the righteous would rejoice and the wicked would have to answer for their sins.

4

Jesus' Messianic Awareness

The quest of the historical Jesus has reached a most interesting stalemate. On the one hand we are more than ever sure that Jesus did not say he was the Messiah. A large body of scholars, building on this sure foundation, have concluded that Jesus neither claimed nor thought of himself as Messiah. On the other hand the discovery of the Dead Sea Scrolls and the renewed attention to the writings of Josephus have brought into high relief the multitude of messianic expectations that engrossed the attention of most Jews in the Holy Land and beyond in the crucial century before the Fall of Jerusalem. The growing certainty that messianism was not Jesus' intention chimes badly with the evidence that everyone else seemed to be agog with expectation of the coming of the Messiah.

The silence of Jesus cannot, in my view, be denied. A good example is the scene before the High Priest recorded in Matthew 26.59-66; Mark 14.55-64; Luke 22.71. The High Priest (in Matthew and Mark) and the whole Sanhedrin (in Luke) are reported as asking Jesus directly whether he was the Messiah. In Matthew and Luke he replies, "You say that I am." Only in Mark does he say, "I am." However, there are textual variants. The Koridethi Codex; the group of late manuscripts identified by William Hugh Ferrar of Trinity College, Dublin in the nineteenth century as forming a "family", called Family 13 after its most prominent member; the important manuscripts numbered 565 and 700; together with the Georgian and Armenian translations of the New Testament read the longer text, *You say that I am*. Although the Greek manuscripts that support the longer reading are all ninth century or later, they represent readings that were current long before. The manuscripts that modern translations of the New Testament rely upon are mostly the result of the great editorial work that was carried out by the church in Alexandria in the fourth century to purify and standardise the text of the canon. Before printing, all copies were made individually and the copyists, being human, usually managed to make mistakes in their work, so that the Bible could read rather differently in different parts of the church as the tiny mistakes were propagated by subsequent copyists. The Alexandrian standardisation was largely successful, but the scholars responsible for the work were not infallible, and some of their decisions are questionable.

Fortunately we possess later manuscripts that were descendants of manuscripts produced before the work of standardisation had been accomplished, so that we are able to peep into the workshops of the standardisers and see some of the array of variants on which they had to decide. They worked by rules of textual criticism that are still employed today, rules like *Prefer the shorter reading* and *Prefer the harder reading*. There is sense in these rules, since it is a well-known tendency to write in extra words that seem called for by the context, and to smooth out wording that seems obscure or difficult. But the rules do not always produce a correct result. A shorter reading may be the result of an accidental omission; a hard reading may be the result of corruption and be too hard to maintain.[1]

In the case of Jesus' answer to the High Priest in Mark 16.62, we may suspect that a copyist would have thought that *You say that I am* was too indefinite and that Jesus would not have missed the opportunity to make a ringing affirmation of his status. Furthermore, if Matthew and Luke had been aware of Jesus' affirmation that he was the Messiah, they would hardly have been likely to muffle it by giving *You say that I am* in its place.

What about *You say that I am?* Paul Billerbeck (1853-1932), in the large commentary on the New Testament which is still an indispensable source for a wide range of rabbinic parallels to New Testament ideas, argued that this expression meant *Yes*. Geza Vermes and David Daube, two scholars who have worked in the same field with outstanding success, have ventured to disagree with him.[2]

The matter turns on the interpretation of a rabbinic story told about Simon the Modest (who flourished about the end of the first century). Simon the Modest had disputed Rabbi Eliezer's opinion, and the opinion of someone who believed they had the High Priest's ruling, that no one could enter a certain gate of the Temple (which, of course, was no longer in existence) with unwashed hands and feet. He cited his own experience. He had entered unchallenged although unwashed. To Rabbi Eliezer's taunt, Who is of more value, you or the High Priest? Simon answered nothing. Rabbi Eliezer retorted that Simon was of less importance than the High Priest's dog, which would

---

[1] O'Neill (1989b).
[2] Vermes (1973), pp. 148-149; Daube (1994), pp. 325-330.

have been turned back it if had ventured to enter unwashed, so that Simon's view was of no value, didn't he know? Simon, true to his name, replied, "You say so." Billerbeck thought that that reply meant Yes; Vermes and Daube, rightly in my view, argue that Simon was simply reserving his own judgment.

Even in reply to Peter's confession that Jesus was the Messiah, there is no record of a positive endorsement, in Mark's Gospel at least. In Mark we simply have a report of the general tenor of Jesus' reply—he commanded them to tell no one about himself *or* about this. The absence of a saying of Jesus shows that the evangelist did not possess any report of Jesus' words on the subject. The evangelist assumed that Jesus affirmed the truth of Peter's reply, but he lacked the evidence of a statement of Jesus to this effect.

The position seems different in Matthew. There Jesus is reported as replying, "Blessed are you, Simon bar Jonah, for flesh and blood have not revealed this to you but my Father in heaven" (Matt 16.17).

This saying raises an interesting issue where a better understanding of Jewish customs helps us to come to a more accurate account of the events that the New Testament reports. It has been the custom among scholars to think that their job in studying the reported sayings of Jesus is to decide between sayings as to whether they are authentic or not. These scholars rightly discerned that, in the process of transmission, the text has been brought into closer conformity with the mature faith of the second-century church. An example is the corruption of the text of Jesus' answer to the High Priest from *You say that I am* to *I am* discussed above. They have tried to eliminate all the sayings of Jesus that agree strongly with established Christian doctrine and to regard as authentic only those sayings that would go against the grain of later Christian teachers. Similarly, they have tried to eliminate all sayings that fit in with Judaism on the grounds that the first scribes and teachers were steeped in Judaism and would have unconsciously attributed to Jesus Jewish teaching that fitted in with their own background. So they cast doubt on the authenticity of Jesus' saying, *Do not think that I have come to destroy the Law or the Prophets. I have not come to destroy but to fulfil* (Matt 5.17). Only when they are convinced that the words are distinctive, conforming neither to established church teaching nor to inherited Judaism, could they be certain that they were in touch with the genuine teaching of Jesus.

The trouble about this procedure is that it rather ruthlessly extrapolates from two undoubted facts—that Jesus offended some of his hearers by his teaching, and that Jesus' words were sometimes found difficult to follow in the early church—and so ends up with a Jesus who fits nowhere.

A more serious difficulty is that the scholars who run this line are ignoring what we know about the transmission of the sayings of revered teachers in Judaism. The whole literature of Judaism—the Mishnah and the Tosephta, the two Talmud commentaries on the Mishnah, that of Babylon and that of Jerusalem, the midrashic commentaries on the Bible called Targums and much else—is full of opinions and rulings that are controversial and controverted. The steady ethos of this way of dealing with religious questions was to accept the scriptures as given, however difficult they might be to understand; to treasure the attempts to interpret the scriptures of all the teachers who have engaged in the enterprise, however contradictory they might be; and to continue the debate on the principle that nothing must be added to, nothing omitted, nothing changed in the sacred writings, with the proviso that all commentary is free and valuable. In such an atmosphere it is highly unlikely that anyone deliberately made up words for Jesus to say. Paul captured exactly this spirit when he carefully distinguished between his own opinion and a word of the Lord in 1 Cor 7.10-13.

At the most scribes may have put ancient sayings on the lips of Jesus. We may suspect that most of the occasions in which Jesus is reported as quoting the Old Testament are later attributions to him of scriptural statements that he would have endorsed. I would argue that the famous words from the cross, where Jesus is reported as quoting the opening of Psalm 22, *My God, my God, why have you forsaken me?* falls into this category. Far from being a shocking statement that the church would want to get rid of, this is more likely to be an attribution to Jesus of words of his father David, words which perfectly fitted the situation. The scribe who added this quotation from the Psalm would have understood the prayer as the obedient prayer of the Messiah who asks the question because he is sure of the answer: the Messiah had to be forsaken by his Father in order to bear fully the sins of a humanity that had cut itself off from God by sin.

I would conclude that no whole sayings of Jesus are inauthentic except sayings that come from before he was born, and those mostly from the Hebrew Bible.

Yet there are sayings containing inauthentic features left. Here is an obvious example from the Gospel of Thomas.

He who blasphemes against the Father will be forgiven, and he who blasphemes against the Son will be forgiven; but he who blasphemes against the Holy Spirit will not be forgiven, either on earth or in heaven. (Logion 44)

It is obvious that the doctrine of the Trinity has shaped this saying; and explicit church teaching has been read back onto Jesus' saying about the sin against the Holy Spirit. We can easily remove the corruptions and regain the original saying. But wait a minute. The idea of a *sin against the Holy Spirit* looks very much like a church-idea too, meaning: You can criticise Jesus but don't think you can challenge accredited church teachers who possess the Holy Spirit, and still get away with it. I suspect that even the version in our canonical Gospels has been corrupted by scribes, and that Jesus originally said something like this: "All sins will be forgiven, except sins against this spirit" (cf. Matt 12.31-31; Mark 3.38-30; Luke 12.10).

Jesus was originally teaching the hard-hearted not to treat others as though they were beyond the pale and incapable of forgiveness; they might find themselves before God in desperate need of forgiveness and hear the inexorable saying, *Unless you forgive you will not be forgiven.*[3] In other words, Jesus' saying has been progressively corrupted by small additions. The word *spirit* almost inevitably prompted the addition of the word *holy*; and the words *Holy Spirit* almost inevitably turned a statement about *the sons of men* into a statement about *the Son of Man*, the second person of the Trinity, and so on.

The safe rule to follow, then, is not to decide between authentic sayings and inauthentic sayings (except in obvious quotations from the Old Testament) but to decide between inauthentic features and the authentic core.

Let us now return to Jesus' reply in Matthew's Gospel to Peter's confession of faith in him as the Messiah. The end part of the saying, *but my Father in heaven* is an obvious gloss; a genuine saying of Jesus that flesh and blood had not revealed Jesus' messiahship to Peter has been glossed by a pious scribe who naturally understood that the revelation must have come straight from God the Father. But what would the core statement of Jesus have meant? It cannot have been meant to exclude the sort of witness made to Jesus' messiahship by John the Baptist. *Flesh and blood* must be an idiomatic way speakers used to refer to themselves; *this* flesh and blood has not revealed it to you. In other words, Jesus is blessing Peter—he is going to need all the blessing he

---

[3] O'Neill (1983), 37-42.

can get if he dares to say that Jesus is the Messiah—but reaffirming that the confession cannot have been based on any explicit teaching Peter had received from his master. Jesus is insisting on his own silence on the matter, and warning Peter that he has to take full responsibility for the confession he has just made.

If the Synoptic Gospels, on close examination, contain no certain evidence that Jesus ever said that he was Messiah, the case seems very different with the Fourth Gospel. This Gospel is full of open and direct affirmations of Jesus' messiahship and, indeed, of his membership of the Trinity. Surely here, the reader will be tempted to say, the rule just expounded that no one would wittingly make up sayings of Jesus must break down. Surely the *I am* sayings, for instance, are the creation of someone in the early church.

I concede that the sayings attributed to Jesus in John's Gospel which make such open and direct claims to messiahship are very much in the style of the Prologue and of the statements attributed to John the Baptist in John 3.31-36. They are written in a distinct poetic style rather different from the sort of poetic style found in Jesus' statements in the Synoptic Gospels. In fact this very same contrast can be found in John's Gospel itself. Contrast John the Baptist's sort of poetry, just the sort of poetry the Jesus of the Synoptic Gospels spoke:

> The one who has the bride is the bridegroom.
> The friend of the bridegroom
> who stands and hears him
> rejoices at the voice of the bridegroom.
> He must increase;
> I must decrease. (John 3.29)

with the poetry of a revelatory discourse from John's Gospel, in this case a revelatory discourse attributed to John the Baptist:

> He who comes from above is above all;
> he who is from the earth is of the earth
> and he speaks of the earth.
> He who comes from heaven is above all. (John 3.31)

This is simple and effective poetry in lines, a *revelatory discourse*. Where did it come from? The usual answer by conservative as well as radical scholars is, From the evangelist. I doubt it.

In the example just quoted, the imagery used in the first speech by John the Baptist is of the rising of the sun and the setting of the moon; no self-denigration is involved, for John recognises his essential part in the drama as the one who accompanies the bridegroom and sees the successful marriage with the bride (symbolically Israel) accomplished. The imagery of the revelatory discourse, on the other hand, is imagery of stark opposition between the lower (*from the earth*) and the higher (*from heaven*). The discourse could hardly have been written as commentary on John the Baptist's saying. It looks very much as though the discourse was already in existence and was simply inserted by a compiler who observed the mechanical correspondence between *rising* and *setting*, *above* and *below* in each saying.

But if the discourse was already in existence, where did it come from? Bultmann long ago remarked on the similarity between the discourses and the religious literature of the *Odes of Solomon* and of the sacred books of the Mandaeans. Both sets of writings, in my opinion, were written independently of the canonical Gospels. Bultmann himself held that some of the revelatory material was older than Jesus, although he also held that the evangelist played a crucial role in putting the material into the present form. I think he was right on the first count, but wrong on the second. All the material had been written down, as revelations of what seers had heard when, like the seers in Revelation, they were granted in vision auditory revelations from the glorified Son of Man. The compilers of John's Gospel were simply taking sayings that already existed, and which were perhaps even known as such to many of their readers, and putting them on the lips of Jesus. The original seers believed that the heavenly Son of Man they saw in vision was the Teacher of Righteousness who had suffered a violent death at the hand of his enemies. In vision they heard him say to his heavenly Father, "I have glorified you on earth; I have completed the work you gave me to do" (John 17.4). The compilers of John's Gospel were in effect arguing: Look, the reports of our seers of what they heard the heavenly Son of Man say have been fulfilled. Jesus was that one incarnate and, although (as you know) he did not say openly who he was, the words of the heavenly Son of Man are the key to what he was about and may legitimately now be put on his lips.

John's Gospel gives no comfort to those who would like to find genuine sayings of Jesus in which he claims to be Messiah. It is interesting to note that Origen, the third-century teacher and scholar, saw evidence in John's Gospel itself for the silence of Jesus.

> We may also notice that it was a habit of Jesus everywhere to avoid speaking about himself. That is why he said: "If I speak of myself, my witness is not true." (John 5.31) And since he avoided speaking about himself, and wanted to show that he was Christ rather by his deeds than by his talk, on

this account the Jews say to him: "If thou art the Christ tell us plainly." (John 10.24) (*Contra Celsum* 1.48)[4]

It seems that Origen recognised that the revelatory discourses of Jesus in that Gospel were not actual reports of Jesus' words.

Even the *hints* of messiahship disappear on close examination. For example, Jesus is reported as having given two answers to those who wanted him to rebuke the woman who anointed his feet with precious ointment, who wanted him to say to her that the ointment should have been sold and the proceeds given to the poor. The first answer is:

> The poor you always have with you; but me you do not always have. (Matt 26.11; Mark 14.7; John 12.8)

The second answer is given in three forms:

> She acted in view of my burial in pouring this myrrh on my body. (Matt 26.12)
> She has anointed my body beforehand for burial. (Mark 14.8)
> Let her be, for she has observed this against the day of my burial. (John 12.7)

Clearly the scene has raised messianic questions. A woman using oil must have suggested that she believed him to be the Messiah. The questioners wanted him to disown the woman and the possible symbolic significance of her action. Jesus in his second answer neatly turns the situation. He does not deny the messianic expectation by rebuking the woman, but nor does he accept the confession. Instead, he uses the symbolism to teach that he is destined to die and to be buried.

In the first answer, however, he clearly accepts the messianic significance of the woman's gesture and argues that the needs of the poor can wait, for he would only be on earth a short time and his messianic dignity should be acknowledged openly, whatever the cost. If that were a genuine saying of Jesus, he would be hinting clearly enough that he was the great King, the Messiah. Observe, however, that the words are a clear reminiscence of a saying from Deuteronomy:

> If there be among you a poor man of one of thy brethren within any of thy gates in the land which the Lord thy God giveth thee, thou shalt not harden thine heart, nor shut thine hand from thy poor brother: but thou shalt open thine hand wide unto him, and shalt surely lend him sufficient for his need, in that which he wanteth... For the poor shall never cease out of the land: therefore I command thee, saying, Thou shalt open thine hand

---

[4] Translated by Henry Chadwick (1953), p. 45.

wide unto thy brother, to thy poor and to thy needy, in the land. (Deut 15.7, 8, 11)

The saying attributed to Jesus, *The poor you shall always have with you*, is a clear enough quotation, but a quotation used in just the opposite sense from the original. The original is warning against the excuses people are tempted to make to avoid helping the poor and offering the sober observation that the task of helping the poor has no end; Jesus is said to be advocating a temporary break—after the pressing task of giving proper honour to the Messiah, there will still be plenty of poor left who are in need of help. This looks to me like another example of an Old Testament quotation being attributed to Jesus. Of course the scribe who first made the marginal note to this effect felt, perhaps rightly, that proper honour to the Son of God was supremely important, and the basis of all subsequent help for the poor. Anyone who decides to build a magnificent church and to adorn it with glorious paintings has made a decision on these lines, but it does seem out of character for Jesus himself to say, particularly as we have discovered him to be chary of revealing who he was to anyone. The saying is not, in my opinion, genuine. If it goes, one of the hints of the Messiah goes too.

A very pervasive hint of messiahship is in the frequent reference by Jesus to *my Father* in distinction from *your Father* with reference to the disciples. Since the Messiah was held to be the Son of God, he would stand in a special relation of sonship to God the Father, and the little word *my* nicely conveys this. Here again close attention to the textual tradition of the New Testament throws up evidence that makes me doubt the authenticity of the little word *my*. The expression *my Father* occurs about fifty times, and in all but six cases there is some evidence of omission or of different position from manuscript to manuscript that suggests that the word *my* had been added by scribes, who of course held that Jesus did stand in a special relationship to his Father. In the Gospel of Thomas, which is not directly dependent on any of our canonical gospels but which gives us independent access to the traditions of Jesus' sayings, the word *Father* referring to God occurs fifteen times, but in only two cases (Logions 64, 94) does it read *my Father*; in all other cases it is *the Father*. We should conclude that Jesus always said *the Father* when referring to God—more evidence that the hints of messiahship are later corruptions introduced by scribes.

It has often been taught that Jesus avoided the term *Messiah* because he wanted to avoid the nationalistic and triumphalist notions attached to what are labelled *Jewish* ideas of the Messiah. Instead, it is argued, he adopted a universal and non-Jewish term *Son of Man*.

There are two answers to be made to this line of argument. The first is that there is no evidence that Jesus in any way altered or repudiated the Jewish teaching of the Pharisees that at the coming of the Kingdom of God at the end of this age the Messiah would come as judge to condemn sinners and vindicate the righteous. The Messiah would come to Jerusalem, the city of David, and the Jews would be the first to experience his salvation—and to face his judgment. Judgment would begin with the house of God. But then the Gentiles would also participate in the blessings of the Kingdom, receiving a just and merciful judgment according to their situation (cf. Romans 2). The idea that Jews at this time thought that God condemned Gentiles simply because they were Gentiles is unfounded. The *Testaments of the Twelve Patriarchs*, for example, are full of promises of salvation for the Gentiles as for Israel. The Jewish community in Alexandria used to invite their Gentile friends and neighbours every year to a gigantic picnic on the island of Pharos to celebrate the translation of the Hebrew scriptures into Greek (Philo, *Moses* 2.41-43).[5] Jesus never suggested any different picture. I find no trace in his teaching that he spiritualised the standard teaching about the Kingdom of God in any way that would change its significance for his hearers.[6]

Secondly, the term *the son of man* is a Jewish expression which means *the man* or *a man*. Many of the sayings of Jesus that contain it are simple examples of an idiom that Geza Vermes has done most to remind us of, whereby a speaker refers back to himself. The Greek says, literally, *the son of man*, but that is best translated into English as *a son of man*. A good example is the saying:

> Foxes have holes and birds of the air have nests, but a son of man has nowhere to lay his head. (Matt 8.20; Luke 9.58)

It is not true that all humanity is homeless, and Jesus must be referring to himself.

However, there are other sayings in which *The Son of Man* seems to be a title, as when Jesus is reported as saying that the leaders who were examining him would see the Son of Man sitting at the right hand of power and coming on the clouds of heaven. (Matt 26.64; Mark 14.62; cf. Luke 22.69) The fact that Rabbi Akiba, who backed Bar Cochba during the revolt of 135, explained the plural *thrones* in Daniel 7.9, a

---

[5] Hart (1992), p. 293.
[6] O'Neill (1993b).

passage about one like a son of man, as *one for Him and one for David* (Babylonian Talmud *Hagigah* 14a; *Sanhedrin* 38b) is decisive. Rabbinic tradition was very conservative, and Akiba's interpretation of the passage in Daniel as referring to the Messiah's throne shows that *Son of Man* was an established messianic expression.[7]

How would people distinguish between the two usages? It would not be difficult. Consider sentences in English in which the word *striker* is used. We have no difficulty in telling from context whether the striker in question is a very active person taking part in a ball game or a very passive person refusing to work. Similarly, speakers of Aramaic before the Fall of Jerusalem could usually distinguish between *son of man* referring to anyone or to oneself and *Son of Man* (which would of course sound the same although I have printed it this time with capital letters) who was suffering the destiny laid on him by God or who was acting as Messiah.

If Jesus was using the expression with the first sense, he was making no open or explicit reference to himself as Messiah. But now here is the surprising thing. If Jesus was using the expression in the second sense, he was referring to the Messiah all right, but he was not claiming, either openly or covertly, to be that Messiah. He was simply giving teaching about the Messiah, whoever the Messiah might be.

A good example of how scribes missed the distinction between *a son of man* as an idiom of self-reference and *The Son of Man* as a title for the Messiah can be found in Matthew 16.27; Mark 8.38; Luke 9.26. Matthew has just one saying, a saying that states that The Son of Man is to come in the glory of his Father with his angels and recompense everyone according to their deeds. Clearly a statement about the heavenly Messiah. Mark and Luke have versions of that saying also, but each prefaces it with another saying, which must once have stood alone, *Whoever is ashamed of me and my words, a son of man will be ashamed of him*—or, more likely, *for him*. This is clearly a use of the idiom. A teacher is saying that, if a disciple is ashamed of his teacher and his teaching, that teacher will be ashamed for him on the day of judgment, for the teacher must take some of the blame. Paul said the opposite in 1 Thessalonians 2.19-20, that the Thessalonians who had believed in Christ would be Paul's glory and joy in the presence of Christ at his coming. There is no more of a messianic claim in Jesus' statement than in Paul's.

---

[7] Horbury (1985). This classical article has been thoroughly vindicated by much recent discussion.

Once the two sayings of Jesus, about himself (using the idiom *a son of man*) and about the Messiah (using the title *The Son of Man*) were put together, the question inevitably arises, Is the expression titular in both cases, so that Jesus is claiming to be the Son of Man now and teaching that despising him as Messiah now will lead to judgment by him as Messiah on the day of judgment? That is what the scribe who put the two sayings together must have meant. Or the question is, Does Jesus use the idiom in the first half of the statement in order to distinguish himself sharply from the Messiah in the second half? Bultmann took the second possibility seriously and argued that Jesus distinguished himself from the Son of Man; Jesus actually denied that he was the Messiah, even if he asserted that a decision for or against himself would be decisive on the day of judgment.

Both possibilities arise only because compilers of the sayings of Jesus have artificially made one sentence out of two sayings, originally independent. Jesus did remind his disciples that they would shame their teacher on the day of judgment if they disregarded his teaching, and Jesus did teach that the Son of man would come and judge all according to their lives. The fact that he said both things did not involve him either in affirming or denying that he was the Messiah. Put them together, however, as is done in Mark and Luke, and scholars think that they are bound to read off from the combination either an affirmation that Jesus was the Son of Man, or a denial.

On both counts the hypothesis that Jesus was using the expression *the son of man* to provide a subtle substitute for the current Jewish ideas of the Messiah has been proved false; he neither repudiated nor changed current expectation about the Messiah, and *the son of man* was a current expression to refer to oneself or to convey teaching about the Messiah. That teaching did contain one fairly novel feature, the teaching that the Son of Man, the Messiah, would rise from the dead ahead of the general resurrection, but even that feature was anticipated among some Jewish circles, as can be seen from reading Revelation 11.3-12.[8] Even in this teaching Jesus neither said nor hinted that he was that Son of Man; but, of course, neither did he deny it.

We can understand how scholars have come to the conclusion that Jesus did not think of himself as Messiah and did not want his followers to be concerned about the issue. As a result they have seized on other aspects of Jesus' teaching and made them the clue to understanding what he was getting at. Elisabeth Schüssler Fiorenza gives us a

---

[8] Berger (1976).

Jesus who was a prophet teaching wisdom. Geza Vermes sees his affinities with Galilean rabbis who performed miracles of healing, men like Honi the Circle Drawer and Hanina ben Dosa. Gerald Downing and Burton Mack concentrate on Jesus' ethical teaching and think of him as a Jewish Cynic preacher. John Dominic Crossan paints him as a peasant Jewish Cynic who offered people both free healing and the comfort of being invited to eat at a common table. John Riches sees Jesus as a prophetic figure who spoke for the powerless and looked forward to some act of divine intervention. Marcus J. Borg sees Jesus as a charismatic healer who founded a prophetic movement which tried to structure society according to the politics of compassion. There is some truth in all these pictures, but they share the one universal feature: they all assume that messiahship was not at the centre of Jesus' interests. John P. Meier reports on an "unpapal conclave" of a Catholic, a Protestant, a Jew, an agnostic, all honest historians, locked up till they emerge with a consensus about Jesus. So far, Jesus is a travelling healer with good news for the poor about a coming kingdom of God that is also here: a marginal Jew, on collision course with the Jerusalem priesthood. There was a family connection with David, but messianic expectation seems to have nothing to do with his death.[9]

The trouble is, the more we find out about Judaism of the time, the more interest we find in the Messiah. While non-messianic lives of Jesus pop up like mushrooms in one paddock, messianic histories of Judaea before the Fall of Jerusalem pop up like mushrooms in the other paddock. Leaving aside the prophets, what were all the other popular leaders in Josephus doing but pretending to be kings: Ezekias and his family (Judas, son of Ezekias also called Judas the Galilean; Menahem; and Eleazar, son of Jair); Simon the former slave of Herod; Athronges the shepherd; John of Gischala; Simon bar Giora; and Jonathan of Cyrene? And what was a pretended king doing but hoping to be the son of David, the Messiah, who would liberate Israel from all foreign domination and bring in the Kingdom of God?

The story of Ezekias (Hezekiah, Hiskia) and his family is instructive. During the time of Julius Caesar's rule in Rome, the Idumean king Antipater gained the local suzerainty in Judaea. His son Herod (Herod the Great) first showed his rashness and ruthlessness in capturing Ezekias, head of a large band of followers in Galilee, and summarily putting him to death. The Sanhedrin haled him before them because

---

[9] Schüssler Fiorenza (1983); Vermes (1973); Downing (1987; 1988; 1992); Mack (1988; 1993); Crossan (1991; 1993); Riches (1980); Borg (1987; 1994); Meier (1991; 1994; and see Hills [1998]).

he executed a Jew without trial, but Herod overawed them and eventually suspended their sitting. He had to be dissuaded by his father and brother from taking Jerusalem with his armed forces. Now Ezekias, the leader he had executed, bore the name of the King of Judah at the time of the prophet Isaiah who had restored temple worship, destroyed the golden serpent because it was becoming an object of worship, and invited Israel to celebrate a purified passover (2 Kings 18-20). He was probably seen as a type of the Messiah. Rabbi Hillel said there was to be no Messiah for Israel because they had enjoyed him during the days of Hezekiah. Johanan ben Zakkai as he lay dying said, "Prepare a throne for Hezekiah the King of Judah who is coming." Some rabbis took these statements as referring to Ezekias, the man killed by Herod. That belief is interesting, because it shows people thinking that a dead leader could return as Messiah.

Ezekias had a son called Judas who raised a large band of followers, broke open the royal arsenals and attacked other aspirants to power (Josephus *War* 2.56; *Ant* 17.271-272). He is probably the Judas of Galilee who founded what Josephus called The Fourth Philosophy. Judas taunted his people for paying taxes to the Romans and tolerating them as their rulers when their ruler should be God alone (Josephus *War* 2.118; *Ant* 18.4-10, 23-25). Judas the Galilean and another similar leader called Theudas were referred to by Gamaliel in Acts 5.37 as messianic pretenders.

Judas's son (or grandson) Menahem, at the time of the Jewish revolt against Rome in 66, led his followers to Masada and broke into Herod's armoury in order to arm them. He advanced on Jerusalem as king and directed the siege of the palace in Jerusalem. Eventually he occupied the Temple with his armed followers, and appeared arrayed in royal robes—some said, with gold working on the linen (Josephus *War* 2.444). Eliazar ben Ananias turned the Zealots against him and, though he fled and hid himself, he was discovered and murdered. A relative, another Eliazar, captured the fortress Masada, and eventually perished there during the Roman siege (Josephus *War* 7.275-406). Later Jewish tradition said that the name of the Messiah was Menahem (Babylonian Talmud *Sanhedrin* 98b), perhaps a reference to Menahem the son of Judas the Galilean.

Here is a whole dynasty devoted to putting themselves forward as king in order to restore the sole lordship of God over his people and to remove foreign rule. Who else could these people have thought they were than possible Messiah?

The recent excavation of Masada, the renewed interest in the writings of Josephus on the part of Ed Sanders and his pupil, Rebecca Gray, the discovery of a War Scroll at Qumran, have all made us more aware of the liberation movements that flourished in Judaea at the time. The statement that "the expectation of a messiah was not the rule" in the face of the massive evidence for the universal and general expectation of the restoration of Jerusalem, the city of David, produced by the very author responsible for that judgment, one who has done so much to help us to read Josephus with new attention, is most surprising and cannot stand as a verdict on these times.[10]

What is the bearing of this research into Jewish thought before the Fall of Jerusalem on the history of Jesus? In the end, every attempt to explain why Jesus was put to death has to bring in the factor that the authorities believed that he was a messianic pretender. The superscription on the cross, *King of the Jews*, was unlikely to have been made up by the Christians (Matt 27.37; Mark 15.26; Luke 23.38; John 19.19, 21). Even Geza Vermes, who rightly emphasizes that Jesus never asserted that he was the Messiah and who has produced another plausible role for Jesus to play, has to concede that the authorities panicked at the prospect of a popular uprising "which this dangerous Galilean, whom many proclaimed as the son of David, might easily have brought about."[11] The crowds said Jesus was Messiah, even if no one else did.

The recently published scrolls from Cave Four at Qumran on the Dead Sea reinforce the impression that the sectaries were vitally interested in the Messiah. We always knew that they were preparing for the coming Messiah of Aaron and of Israel, a Kingly Messiah who was also a Priestly Messiah (1QS 9.11 [the only plural form, a plural of majesty]; 1QSa 2.12, 14, 20; 1Q30 1 1.2(?); 4Q Patriarchal Blessings (4Q252) 5.3; 11Q Melchizedek 2.18; CD [Cairo Damascus Document] 2.12; 12.23-13.1; 14.19; 19.10; 20.1; 6Q15 3.4). The one mystery seemed to be that this Messiah was not mentioned in the War Scroll, but it seems likely that he is in fact there, as the Glorious Man, the Lord who is a Man of War (1QM 12.10-15). He is described in terms used of Judah in Genesis 49.8.

The phrase *Son of God*, which used to be regarded as the hallmark of the christology of the later hellenistic church, has turned up in 4Q246. It is no longer possible to write off all the references to the

---

[10] Sanders (1992), p. 295 for the statement, and pp. 289-295 for the importance of David and David's city, Jerusalem. Gray (1993).
[11] Vermes (1973), pp. 140, 144.

term *Son of God* and to Psalm 2 as reflections of the later theology of the church. This imagery was an active force in the imagination of Jews in the two centuries before the Fall of Jerusalem.

Let me draw attention to another small piece of evidence for popular interest in the Messiah. It keeps being said that the term for Jesus, *The Nazorean*, and for his followers, *Nazoreans* (with an o in the second syllable in each case), simply derives from the town of Nazareth (with an a in the second syllable), but the story will not wash.[12] The Jewish evidence is decisive. Besides the name of the town and the name given to Jesus and his followers, in later Jewish writings there is a different word again, with the long o in the first syllable instead of in the second, and with Tsade as the second consonant instead of Zayin. The town of Nazareth was spelt with a Tsade, and there was no o sound in the name anywhere; the popular name for Jesus and his followers was spelt with a Zayin, and the o stood in the second syllable; the later term in the Talmud and elsewhere was spelt with a Tsade and the o stood in the first syllable. That means that there are three words in play: the name of the town, the name well-wishers applied to Jesus and his followers, and the name opponents applied to Jesus and his followers.

Even if we go no further, it is obvious that messianism lies behind the game. A similar play on words occurred in the case of Simon, the leader of the revolt of AD 135. His name was Bar Kosiba; his followers called him Bar Kokhba, *Son of a Star*, after Numbers 24.17; and, when the revolt failed, his enemies called him Bar Koziba, *Son of the Lie*. They took out the second Kaph from the honorific title and put in Zayin Yod. His real name suggested—but did not supply—the messianic title, and the unhappy outcome of the revolt suggested another way the name could be read. Similarly, for Jesus the town suggested the messianic title, and the opposition he aroused suggested a less than flattering substitute, switching the vowel and substituting a likesounding, but different, consonant.

All this can be deduced from the evidence, without entering into speculation as to what the popular title or the sarcastic metathesis might have meant. But let me go further. Perhaps the title, an adjective or noun *nezori* or *nezor* from the root *nzr* meant *A man for dedication, for consecration, for coronation*. Then the metathesis, an adjective or noun from the root *ntsr*, *notser*, meaning *enemy* (see Jer 4.16), was put

---

[12] Most recently, Barrett (1994), p. 140.

in its place: Jesus was the agent of Beelzebub, The Enemy.[13] If there is anything in this suggestion, it reinforces the impression that whether or not Jesus was the Messiah was an issue from the very beginning of his ministry. It would be a bold critic that denied that Jesus was called *Nazorean* and his followers *Nazoreans*. Once that is conceded, it is conceded that the great issue of his ministry was whether or not Jesus was Messiah. If he did not affirm it, he did not deny it.

The terms *Antichrist* and *Antichrists* reflect ideas much earlier than the New Testament, as Bousset has shown, and they bear witness to the deep and widespread longing for the coming of a Christ and of Christ's followers.[14] They also indicate that it was a popular belief that Satan would try to deceive people by inspiring messianic parodies. The fact that parodies of the Messiah were regarded as possible—Jesus himself is reported as warning against them—shows that the Messiah at his coming would at first be hidden and hard to discern.

Scholars have played the game to reach stalemate. The closer the reading of the sayings of Jesus, the less ground for the assertion that he said he was the Messiah or even hinted he was the Messiah. The better the reading of contemporary Jewish history before the Fall of Jerusalem, the clearer it becomes that everyone was agog as to who was to be Messiah.

Long ago, building on some remarks of that great scholar, David Flusser, I asserted that there was a Jewish law in existence at the time which declared that anyone who claimed in so many words to be the Messiah was guilty of blasphemy and should be put to death. From this law it would follow that, if Jesus held that he was the Messiah, he was forbidden to say so. I also argued that the religious charge against Jesus was that he had in fact stated that he was the Messiah; this was the blasphemy for which he was held worthy of death.[15] Graham Stanton and Craig Evans have most recently—the one orally, at the British New Testament conference at Exeter, September 1993, and the other in print—put the question, Where is the evidence for this law?[16] I have often appealed to John 19.7, *We have a law and by that law he ought to die, because he made himself the Son of God*, and I stand by that. *Son of God* is no longer to be regarded as the substance of the charge, since we now know that *Son of God* was a good Jewish way of referring to

---

[13] New Schürer (1973), pp. 543-544; Vermes (1973), pp. 173-174; O'Neill (1999), pp. 135-142.
[14] Bousset (1895).
[15] O'Neill (1968-69; 1970).
[16] Evans (1995), p. 407, n. 1.

the Messiah. The charge must have lain in the words *he made himself*; anyone who claimed in words to be the Messiah was automatically a blasphemer worthy of death.

The rule is implied in *1 Enoch* 62.7, "For the Son of Man was concealed from the beginning, and the Most High One preserved him in the presence of his power; then he revealed him to the holy and the elect ones." Only when the congregation of the holy ones is planted and the elect stand before him, that is, when the Kingdom comes and the dead are raised and the righteous vindicated, do the kings and governors fall down at his feet begging for mercy (*1 Enoch* 62.8-9).

A mark of the Antichrist was that he would say, "I am God" (Ezek 28.2, 6, 9; Isa 14.13-14; *AscIsa* 4.6; *OrSib* 5.33-34; 2 Thess 2.4; cf. Dan 11.36; Rev 13.4-6). Jesus warned that deceivers would come in [God's] name saying, I am. All our manuscripts report the words of Jesus as follows: "For many will come in *my* name, saying I am [the Messiah]," but we should probably omit *my* by conjecture as the natural addition of scribes who believed that the first coming was over and that they awaited only the second coming of Jesus; during his ministry Jesus himself could not sensibly have assumed that (Matt 24.5; Mark 13.6; Luke 21.8). If anyone claimed to be the Messiah and did not wait for God to reveal his Messiah he would be self-condemned.

Justin Martyr cites his Jewish protagonist Trypho as saying, "But Christ, if he is born and exists somewhere, is unknown and does not know himself nor has any authority until Elijah comes and anoints him and makes him manifest to all" (*Dial* 8.4).

But we need the actual wording of a law that might cover this sort of case, and we need some justification for the existence of such a law, if indeed it exists.

For the actual wording, consider Mishnah, *Sanhedrin* 11.5:

> "The false prophet"—he that prophesies what he has not heard and what has not been told him, his death is at the hands of men; but he that suppresses his prophecy or disregards the words of another prophet or the prophet that transgresses his own words, his death is at the hands of Heaven, for it is written, *I will require it of him*.

Admittedly, the words I want are an aside at the beginning of the substantial point of the law, but they are there. The words, *he that prophesies what he has not heard and what has not been told him* is simply the prohibition of saying what God has not said and includes a prohibition against speaking of something which might be true but the truth of which had not yet been released by God. If the name of the Messiah was not to be spoken by the Messiah himself, then this law would attach the death penalty to that statement. Someone who claimed out loud to be Messiah, even though he held that God had told him he was, would be a false prophet if this news was not to be spoken by the Messiah himself. The day of his manifestation is known only to God, which implies that God alone can make it known (Zech 14.7; *4 Ezra* 13.52; *PsSol* 17.21; *2 Bar* 21.8; Babylonian Talmud *Sanhedrin* 99a; Targum Ecclesiastes 7.24; Matt 24.36; Mark 13.32).

But is there any more direct evidence of such a ruling? It may be found, I believe, in the Epistle to the Hebrews, in a passage that is patently drawing on ancient Jewish teaching. In Hebrews 5.4 the rule is cited that no one takes to himself the honour of being priest, but only one who is called by God is installed in the post, as in the case of Aaron. The writer is referring to the story of the sons of Korah in Numbers 16 who wanted to take on themselves the duties of the priests. In Hebrews 5.5 the argument continues, "So also the Messiah did not glorify himself to become High Priest, but the one who spoke the words to him, You are my son; this day have I begotten you", to give a fairly literal translation. The aorist tense that I have translated *the Messiah did not glorify himself* can, however, hardly be an aorist referring to some time in the past, since no event in the life of the Messiah is being referred to, nor any event in the life of Jesus. The most natural reading is to take the aorist as a gnomic aorist and to translate, *the Messiah is not to glorify himself, but only the one who is to speak to him the words, You are my son; this day have I begotten you*. If so, we have the ruling I had conjectured was in existence in Jerusalem before the fall of that city in AD 70.

What has produced the stalemate in quest of the historical Jesus is, on the one hand, the elimination of every trace from his authentic teaching of messianic claims or even hints of messianic claims, and, on the other hand, the disappearance of the picture of a Judaism that was not much interested in who might be the Messiah. Everyone was looking for the Messiah, and any candidate knew that he had to keep silence concerning just that question, on pain of death.

There is one massive piece of evidence that supports this view. All the evidence we have—from Josephus as well as from the New Testament—indicates that the Messiah would be hard to discern when he came; you would have to look for him, using all the clues you could muster from the Old Testament, and there was no easy way of knowing whether your identification was correct. The people in Josephus's accounts were looking for *the tokens of salvation*, τὰ σημεῖα τῆς σωτηρίας (Josephus, *War* 2.259; 6.205). The phrase recalled the passage in Psalm 89.50-51:

> Remember, Lord, the reproach of thy servants...
> wherewith thine enemies have reproached, O Lord;
> wherewith they have reproached the footsteps of thine anointed.

The footsteps of the Messiah are the burden of one of the two explicit references to the Messiah in the Mishnah, Mishnah *Sotah* 9.15: *With the footprints of the Messiah presumption shall increase and dearth reach its height.* I suggest that the average pious Jew of the time read the story of David and David's Psalms as a clue to what he should expect in his own day: a hidden Messiah and a persecuted Messiah and a Messiah that had to be discerned as such without any direct teaching from the Messiah himself. The days when David, already anointed King over Israel by Samuel, had to hide in the caves from Saul, and the days when King David had to leave Jerusalem during the revolt led by Absalom were taken as indications of how the Messiah would have to behave when he at last came.

That is the explanation of the numerous tests applied to Jesus and John the Baptist in all four Gospels. If Jesus was a sinner, he could not be Messiah; so it was important to know if a sabbath healing was or was not a sin. If anyone knew where he came from, he could not be the Messiah. If he came from Galilee or Nazareth or Samaria, he was unlikely to be the Messiah. If he did not come from Bethlehem, he could not be the Messiah. If he was a lover of wine and good company, he could not be the Messiah; if he was an ascetic, he could not be the Messiah. The crowds could be divided about who he was and Jesus asked his disciples about their speculations. Even someone who had probably been convinced by a vision that Jesus was Messiah could come to doubt and could send messengers to find out if he were. Jesus, of course, could not say he was; all he could say was, *Tell him what you see and hear.* It is probably a pious scribe who supplied the next part of the speech, the allusions to passages from Isaiah (Matt 11.2-6; Luke 7.18-2). The only choice was for everyone to make up their minds on the evidence of what they saw and heard.

The Messiah had to suffer; all were agreed on that, simply because David had to suffer. All the Psalms that referred to the tribulations of the Psalmist were taken as davidic and therefore as messianic. Israel's prayer was, "Lord, remember David and all his afflictions", the opening words of Psalm 132. The Messiah had to suffer in silence; all were agreed on that, simply because it was a rule that the Messiah had to wait for the Father to reveal him: no one was to know the Messiah until the Father disclosed it.

If that is the correct setting for understanding the career of Jesus of Nazareth, what was Jesus thinking all the time? It is a perfectly proper historical question to raise as to what beliefs belonged to the furniture of anyone's mind. We normally raise the question about the general beliefs of a civilization or of an era when we raise such questions as, Did they think that slavery was right? or Did they believe that apartheid was the will of God? Such questions are implicit in perfectly ordinary historical questions such as, When did the average Hungarian functionary begin to see that communism was not going to work? But it is also perfectly proper to raise the question about an individual. Of course, it is not always easy to answer the question, but the question itself is unexceptionable.

Let us start by asking what Jesus believed, without raising the question of what he believed about himself. Since Jesus was a worshipping Jew, he must have shared the beliefs of Jews that God exists, that he is One, that he made the world and made it one, that he continually governs what happens by his providence, and that those who believe this and live by it will have a happy life—the substance of the creed given by Philo in *de opificio mundi* 170-171. Something similar appears in Hebrews 11.6: "But without faith it is impossible to please him: for he that cometh to God must believe that he is, and that he is a rewarder of them that diligently seek him."

Jesus' belief in the providence of God and his rewards must have included an expectation of the full purification and restoration of Jerusalem, the city of David, and the fulfilment of Nathan's prophecy to David that David's son would reign for ever on his throne. As I have argued, Jesus would also have believed, with all Jews, that the Messiah would be hidden at his coming and would have to suffer, like David.

Jesus diverged from universally accepted teaching on the doctrine of the resurrection. Here he sided with the Pharisees and the Essenes against the Sadducees in holding that there would be a general resurrection of the dead at the coming of the Kingdom of God.

That means that he would not have excluded the possibility that the Messiah's sufferings might have to culminate in his death before the general resurrection. This belief was, of course, not open to the Sadducees, but there is evidence that some Jews apart from Jesus held that the Messiah would have to die before the general resurrection. This belief is preserved in a document incorporated into *4 Ezra* (2 Esdras 9.28-33, 36-47; 10.1-4, 15, 17, 18, 24-27a, 29-41, 49, 50) which describes a woman who had a son who died as he entered his bridal chamber, clearly a messianic prophecy. The woman was transfigured in the presence of the seer and uttered a loud and terrifying cry so that the earth was shaken at her voice. She then disappeared (*4Ezra* 10.26, 27a). This looks very like the cry of one who recognises that, with the shaking of the earth, the messianic age is about to come.

I would also argue that the Teacher of Righteousness was held to be the Messiah; that he died by crucifixion; and that he was expected to return at the end of the age as the Messiah of Aaron and Israel.[17]

Jesus would have believed that the Messiah always existed before he was incarnate. He would have shared the belief found in the ancient Jewish tradition preserved in 1 Corinthians 10.4 that the Rock that followed the Israelites on their desert journeys was Christ. We can confirm that this was current Jewish belief by observing that the Ebionites, who denied that Christ was born or died, held that Christ had descended into Jesus at his baptism and had ascended from Jesus before his death (Irenaeus *haer* 1.26.2 [Harvey 1.211-213]; Clementine *Homilies* 3.20; 8.5,6; 16.15). Christ always existed. No one believed that Christ would come into existence at some moment in history. The statement of Peter at Pentecost, "God has made him Lord and Christ, this Jesus whom you crucified" (Acts 2.36) means, *God has installed on his rightful throne as Lord and Christ this Jesus whom you crucified.*

Jesus would therefore also have believed that the Messiah should be worshipped. He would have shared the belief of the seer in Revelation 19.10; 22.8-9 that a person in a human form could be worshipped, but he would also have shared the belief of the angel who sharply told the seer that he, the angel, was not the messiah, only a fellow-servant. The Spirit of prophecy had inspired him and all other fellow-servants to acknowledge Jesus and so to worship God. This looks like a trinitarian belief. Having been brought up in Galilee, Jesus would be well aware of Hellenistic stories about gods taking human form and he would have had to reconcile the belief that the Messiah would come as a human being with his belief that God was One. He would have done so by accepting the trinitarianism that we find in Philo, for example: God is both One and Three (*de Abrahamo* 119-122; *Questions on Genesis* 4.2, 4 &c.). Explaining the appearance of the angels to Abraham on the plains of Mamre, Philo argues that the soul, shone upon by God as if at noonday, perceives a threefold image of one subject, one image of the living God and others of the other two:

---

[17] O'Neill (1991a).

> ...the one in the middle is the Father of the universe, who in the sacred scriptures is called by his proper name, *I am that I am*; and the beings on each side are those most ancient powers which are always close to the living God, one of which is called his creative power, and the other his royal power.

Philo is alluding to the view that there were two Powers in heaven with God, a trinitarian view of God.

Finally, Jesus would believe that the Messiah would be tempted, reading the remark in Isa 28.16 that the stone was a tried or tested stone as proof. That means that he recognized that the Messiah, when he came to earth, would both know that he was the Messiah—for otherwise he would not be acting as the Father's full envoy—and know that he, being fully human, could be wrong. Otherwise he could not be tested and tried and tempted. Jesus would have held the doctrine that the Son of God had to humble himself in order to be born as a human being, a doctrine reproduced in Phil 2.

So far I have simply been imagining what doctrines Jesus was likely to have held, being a Jew alive forty years before the Fall of Jerusalem. He would not have been alone in holding any of the views I have listed, although not all Jews would have held all that he was likely to have held. All would have held that God is One, that the Messiah was to come, that the Messiah was to be hidden and have to suffer; from that point on they would have diverged.

We come, then, to the final question, Did Jesus hold that himself was the Messiah his doctrines led him to expect? There is plenty of evidence that *others* thought he was the expected Messiah or a messianic pretender, but what did he think?

The only way we can decide is by examining the evidence of what he said and what he did. On what he said, there is no statement and no hint. But we must also note that, unlike John the Baptist, he never denied that he was the Messiah. And I have produced an argument that, if he did hold he was the Messiah, he was forbidden by Jewish law to say so.

What about his deeds? Here there seem to be a number of indications that he acted the role of the Messiah. The Messiah was expected, like King David, to cast out evil spirits and to heal—but plenty of other people did that, so that the healings are not decisive. But choosing twelve disciples looks messianic, each disciple representing one of the twelve tribes. Feeding a crowd in the desert looks very like treating them as the desert generation waiting to cross into the Promised Land. Going up to Jerusalem with his disciples at Passover was a messianic thing to do, since the Messiah, in some parts of Judaism, was expected to come at Passover (Mishnah *Pesakim* 10.6; *Mekhilta of Rabbi Joshua ben Hananya* on Ex 12.42; and, as Henry Hart pointed out, the LXX of Jer 38(31).8). Entering Jerusalem on a donkey was also messianic.

Jesus' followers thought that he was the Messiah; the crowds that heard him gladly thought that he was the Messiah; the authorities, both members of the ruling circles of Judaism and Pilate and his entourage, thought that he was a messianic pretender; those who were undecided, like Gamaliel, thought it best to wait and see if he would turn out to be the Messiah. As historians, we should conclude that it is wholly likely that Jesus held that he was the Messiah, too. The absolute silence of Jesus on his messiahship, long regarded as proof that he did not think he was the Messiah, is one more piece of evidence that he did. He seems to have acted deliberately as the incarnate Son of God, above all in going to Jerusalem at Passover to die.

5

The Parables of Jesus

The parables of Jesus cut across two basic tenets of the intelligentsia in the modern world. The first is that morality is only a human construction: we make up our morality by the best means available, either so that our behaviour is according to a rule that is applicable to all everywhere, or so that the probable consequences will be for the best. The second is that we must never act with a view to a reward. Jesus, on the contrary, held that God had given moral rules in the ten commandments which all were bound to obey and that we had to act in order to win the approval of God and his reward.

However, the basic tenets of the intelligentsia were not formed and imposed in opposition to Jesus. On the contrary, the tenets were fashioned by scholars who thought that they were recovering the true import of the teaching of Jesus which the church had distorted and overlaid with the Jewish ideas that Jesus had come to supersede. It was Jesus himself, they argued, who taught that human beings should rise above positive law as given by the sovereign God and should turn their back on an ethics of reward. Jesus was regarded as both a revolutionary and as a religious genius who subverted traditional values.

This modern rewriting of the teaching of Jesus was based on the assumption that the two massive blocks of teaching, the Sermon on the Mount and the Parables, were meant for all people without distinction. The church's traditional understanding, that men and women who lived what is called the "religious" life of poverty, chastity and obedience were the primary target of the Sermon on the Mount, and that the laity who held property, married and were caught up in changeable relations of domination and subservience were the primary target of the Parables. Since this distinction between secular Jews and monastic Jews was already current in Jesus' day, his teaching always took account of the two types of obedience.[1] The rich young ruler, for example, seems, by his persistence, to desire the monastic life of the "perfect", but sadly was not prepared to accept the poverty that was

---

[1] Hamman (1987); O'Neill (1989; 1998).

entailed.[2] When the idea that there were two ways of obedience was finally abandoned at the Reformation, the precepts of the Sermon on the Mount, which are in general possible only for the religious, were either taken literally as imposed on all or were spiritualised in order to be possible for all.[3] This brought in the assumption that the Law of Moses was either superseded by the Sermon on the Mount or was in some sense transcended.

The parables in turn were then taken to be a radical refashioning of Judaism. In them, it was held, the Kingdom of God was redefined and the traditional idea of the law of God as a command, the keeping of which would lead to a future reward in the Kingdom of God, was held to be subverted.

Before I can give what I take to be the true reading of the parables of Jesus, I have to show three things. First, that the parables were not about the Kingdom of God in the sense that they were redefining the meaning of the Kingdom. On the contrary, the parables assume the traditional teaching about the Kingdom as the future coming of the new age when the dead would rise and the righteous would share the joy of the eternal presence of God and the unrighteous would be forever shut out of that felicity.

Secondly, since the parables were designed to prepare people to be fit to enter the Kingdom when it came, they could contain veiled reference to the great actors in the coming of the Kingdom. The figure of a father could stand for God the Father; the figure of a king could stand for the King of Glory, either the Lord of hosts or the Messiah; the figure of a son could stand for the Son of God; and the figure of a bridegroom could stand for the Son of God, the Messiah. This cuts across the general rule, usually maintained by scholars since Jülicher, that the parables were not allegories. It also contradicts the position of Jeremias that no one in Jesus' day would have understood these typological meanings.[4]

Thirdly, some of the parables have been reinterpreted in the New Testament in order to depict the life and activity of the church. That is an understandable process, but Jesus himself seems to have meant the parables for anyone in Israel who would listen. However much I disagree with Jülicher, Dodd, and Jeremias, I accept fully their general observation that the present contexts of the parables in the Gospels

---

[2] O'Neill (1998), pp. 123-125.
[3] Luther (1532), WA 32, pp. 299-301; Works, pp. 3-6.
[4] Jülicher (1899), vol. I, pp. 187-194; 322 *et passim*; Jeremias (1947; Eng. trans., 1963), "the son", pp. 72-73; "the bridegroom", pp. 52-53.

should be disregarded. The contexts are either accidental or represent the evangelists' interpretation, and we cannot assume that the evangelists correctly understood Jesus' intention.

When we strip away these three misunderstandings, we are in a position to see the true nature of the parables of Jesus. In general, they fall into three groups. In the first group, Jesus uses pictures of admirable and not-so-admirable people in order to help his hearers to apply to their own lives the moral judgment that they so easily make on the actors in stories of human situations. In the second group, Jesus uses pictures of the prudent and imprudent choices people make every day in order to sharpen the hearers' wits to make the same sort of prudent choices and avoid the same sort of imprudent choices in relation to the day of judgment when the Kingdom of God would come. In the third group Jesus used metaphors for the spiritual message he wanted to convey; for example, the light of the body is the eye (No. 8 in the Table on pp. 112ff.). This message was strictly governed by traditional Jewish beliefs about the Kingdom of God.

The Three Misunderstandings of the Parables

The Parable of the Leaven (No. 31) is taken as a key to Jesus' understanding of the Kingdom of God. The argument is that Jesus either completely reinterpreted traditional notions, or at least shifted the emphasis away from the future to the present. In traditional Jewish teaching the Kingdom of God was held to be the coming, at the end of history, of a time when all the kingdoms and states of the world would be abolished and God alone would rule over both the living and the dead who had been raised from the dead. Jesus, it is argued, taught "realized eschatology", or "an eschatology that is in the process of realization."[5] This argument was based on the false assumption that when Jesus said, "The Kingdom of God is like leaven" he meant that the Kingdom itself was even then entering into society and spreading its influence as pervasively as leaven permeated the lump of dough in which it was mixed.

---

[5] "Realized eschatology" was most notably taught by Harnack and Dodd; see Harnack (1900; Eng. trans., 1904), pp. 61-64: "Here we have the first complete transition to the conception of the kingdom of God as the power that works inwardly", p. 62; Dodd, (1935; 1961 ed.), p. 41. The more careful term, "an eschatology that is in process of realization" was coined by Haenchen and adopted by Jeremias, with the concurrence of Dodd; Jeremias (1947; Eng. trans., 1963), p. 230. See the wise remarks on Dodd by B.T.D. Smith (1937), p. 78, n. 1.

When a Jewish teacher said, "The Kingdom is like...", he did not mean that the Kingdom was like the first term of the story that followed. He meant, rather, that the important matter of when and how the Kingdom would come, and the important matter of how anyone could be sure of entering the Kingdom when it came was illuminated by the story as a whole. The version of the Parable of the Leaven which is found in the Coptic Gospel of Thomas begins, "The Kingdom of the Father is like a woman..." This version conveys the same message, and of course the Kingdom is no more like a woman than it is like leaven. Similarly, the Parable of the Wise and Foolish Virgins (No. 51), which begins, "Then the Kingdom of Heaven will be compared with ten virgins ...," does not teach that the Kingdom itself is at all like ten young women.

Joachim Jeremias, one of the greatest interpreters of the Parables of Jesus, well understood that the Kingdom was not being directly compared with the first term of the story, but he wrongly went on to argue that the Kingdom was like some other component of the story: "the Kingdom of God is, of course, not 'like a merchant', but like a pearl; ... it is not 'like a king', but like a marriage feast ... the Kingdom of God is not compared to the grain of mustard seed, but to the tall shrub in whose boughs the birds make their nests ... the Kingdom of Heaven in not 'like leaven', but like the prepared risen dough ..."[6] Nevertheless it is highly unlikely that Jesus' hearers would expect any new teaching about the nature of the Kingdom when Jesus told a story that began, "The Kingdom is like..." The Kingdom was the coming age when God would have overthrown all enemies and would rule over the vindicated righteous. The story which began, "The Kingdom is like" or "The Kingdom shall be compared to" would be designed to help the listeners to prepare themselves to enter the Kingdom when it came. By paying attention to the story, the listeners would be alerted to what had to be done in their lives in order to be ready for the coming of the Kingdom. Jeremias, and many other scholars, have been mislead by the argument of Gustav Dalman that the term "The Kingdom" referred to the rule or reign of God in general rather than to the specific state of affairs when God would have bought the history of the present age to an end by introducing the age to come in which all human beings would be judged and his will would be done by all.[7]

The second misunderstanding of the parables has arisen from the paucity of Jewish writings of the time. Scholars like Jeremias concluded

---

[6] Jeremias (1947; Eng. trans., 1963), pp. 101-102.
[7] O'Neill (1993b).

from the seeming absence of evidence that terms like *Father* and *Son* and *Bridegroom* were used to refer to God and his Messiah that the parables that depicted these figures could not have had any such reference. The discovery and publication of the Dead Sea Scrolls and a more careful search of other Jewish writings from the time have thrown up evidence that these images of God and the Messiah were current in Jesus' day.[8] Of course the parables that depicted these figures were not conveying new information about God and the Messiah, and not overturning the traditional teaching. The stories were to help the hearers to be ready for the coming of God and his Messiah, so that the main interest in the allegorical stories was concentrated in the people who had to do with the father and the son and the bridegroom.

The third misunderstanding has found a place in the text of the New Testament. Parables that were told by Jesus in order to help people to prepare for the coming of the Kingdom were glossed in the Gospels by scribes who understood them as giving guidance to church leaders or church members. Thus the Parable of the Lost Sheep (No. 39) in Matt 18.10 was applied to church leaders by comparing them to the shepherd who left the ninety-and-nine sheep in order to seek and find the one that was lost. Of course, the shepherd was also taken to refer to Christ in Matt 18.11 and in the Lucan version (cf. Ps 119.176), but the anachronism of that interpretation is evident when we notice that Luke's setting is Jesus' defence against the charge that he ate with sinners. The lost sheep did not sit down at table with the shepherd and his friends when he had been found and brought back to the fold. The parable is more likely to be a reminder to the hearers to recall the great efforts they would go to, like the shepherd, to find just one lost sheep. If they took so much trouble about one sheep, and thought it worth throwing a party to celebrate the recovery of that sheep, should they not take even more trouble about the one thing that was lacking in their lives if they were to be worthy to enter the Kingdom of God?

More prominently, the long interpretation appended to the Parable of the Sower (No. 28) whereby the different soils on which the seed is scattered are compared with the different states of spiritual receptivity in the hearers of the Word can scarcely be what Jesus meant by the story. The interpretation presupposes that the different kinds of soil (the trodden path; the stony ground; weed-infested ground; and good soil) could choose to be that sort of soil. But the soils in the parable,

---

[8] On God as Father in Judaism, see Isa 63.16; Jer 3.4-5, 19-20; Sir 23.1, 4; 51.10; *TLevi* 17.2; Eusebius *praep. ev.* 8.13. On the Messiah as Son of God and Bridegroom, see O'Neill (1988), pp. 485-486.

even if they understood their nature, could not change it. The parable was probably originally meant to encourage the hearers to go about the matter of preparing themselves for the coming of the Kingdom in the same way as sowers, despite all the difficulties of their task, went about planting a crop.

Stories of admirable and not-so-admirable people

A surprising number of the parables are stories of admirable people, and the admirable people are frequently set off against not-so-admirable people (Class A in the Table of the Parables). The model for this group of about thirty-seven of the parables listed in the Table was the parable told by the Prophet Nathan to King David when he had committed adultery with Bathsheba and arranged for her husband Uriah the Hittite to be killed in battle after Uriah had refused to go to his house and sleep with his wife when David had had him recalled from the front line (the incident: 2 Sam 11; Nathan's parable: 2 Sam 12.1-14). Nathan told David a story about a rich man who received a visitor and, instead of killing and dressing a lamb from his own great flocks for the feast of welcome, went and took the one ewe lamb belonging to the poor man, a lamb which the poor man had bought and reared, which was fed from his own table and lay in his bosom and was as a daughter to him. David was angry and swore by the Lord that the rich man who had done this should be put to death. The prophet then said to David, "Thou art the man."

Jesus' parables similarly often feature an admirable person or an despicable person, and sometimes a contrast between someone whom the hearers would praise and someone whom the hearers would despise. The emotions aroused by the hearers as they entered sympathetically into the action of the story naturally aroused reflection about the hearers' own moral behaviour in analogous situations. No sensible person would build on the sand instead of on the rock (No. 16); nor would any sensible people neglect to make God's commandments the foundation of their lives. We all deplore children who will not join in the games their mates are getting up in the market place, whether Weddings or Funerals (No. 23); but perhaps we are equally reluctant to respond to teaching about the joy of the spiritual wedding or the sorrow of death with its reminder that we must all die. We admire the sower who sets to work to avoid the hazards of farming by preparing good soil and making sure that his seed is not wasted (No. 28); but we are lethargic about our own lives when the reward would be abundant life in the Kingdom of God. We recognize the sense of leaving the tares to grow up with the wheat, for then it is possible to make a separation (No. 29); but we are impatient with what we think our enemies are doing to us and unwilling to wait for God's good time when the issues will be much clearer. We admire the farmer who sows the mustard seed and waits for it to grow into a great bush (No. 30) or the woman who goes to great trouble to keep her dishes clean and who kneads a little leaven into a great mass of dough (No. 31) but we are reluctant to take the tiny steps that will lead to the reward of eternal life for ourselves. We envy the man who found buried treasure in the field he was ploughing, kept his find secret and bought the field (No. 32), and we admire the merchant who sold everything in order to buy the pearl of great price (No. 33), but we remain strangely lethargic when we could get a place in the Kingdom of God, which is a much better reward than either the treasure or the pearl. Of course our fishing net will catch fish we have to throw back into the sea, but that does not deter the fisherman from casting the net (No. 34; cf. No. 89); why do we hesitate to make the effort required to catch the great prize of entry into the Kingdom of God? We go to a prosperous householder and expect him to be able to produce from the storehouse good things, both new and old (No. 35), but we are reluctant to go to God and to ask him for the good things he surely has gathered together in order to supply our greatest needs.

Often there are characters in the parable whom we instinctively condemn. The servant who petitions his master to cancel a great debt and who then refuses the petition of a fellow-servant who makes a similar petition over a comparatively trifling amount cannot but arouse our condemnation (No. 40). Perhaps the story will make us reflect that we often act just like that servant in relation to the merciful God and our fellow human beings who ask us for mercy. We perhaps share the anger of the labourers in the vineyard who have worked hard all through the long hard day and find that the labourers who were only called in for the last hour get exactly the same wage as us (No. 41). Far from showing an absolute contrast between "the world of merit, and the world of grace; the law contrasted with the gospel",[9] this parable both encourages people to work for entry into the Kingdom, even at the eleventh hour, and warns those who have spent their lives working for entry into the Kingdom not to despise the late-comers. The late-comers had in fact worked one hour. We all despise the son who says

---

[9] Jeremias (1947; Eng. trans., 1963), p. 139.

he will obey his father and then does not go to work in the field and admire the son who says he will not obey his father and then does go and work in the field (No. 42). Why, then, do we place such store on professions of godliness and pay so little attention to those who make no profession but do what God requires?

The parable known as the Parable of the Wicked Husbandmen in the Synoptic Gospels seems to be the combination of two parables.[10] One was a parable about the owner of a vineyard who, after several vain attempts to collect the rent, sent his son, whom the tenants of the vineyard killed. This parable was preserved in the Gospel of Thomas (No. 43). This parable was known to the compilers of each of the three Synoptic Gospels, and they combined it with a second parable, about the owner of a vineyard whose tenants repeatedly refused to pay the rent to the servants whom he sent. In the end he came himself and threw out the tenants and installed others who would pay the rent (No. 44). Both parables were realistic, and in both cases the hearers would also have seen the allegorical point. The owner of the vineyard was God the Father. He showed his goodness by sending his Son, whom the tenants killed. The suffering and possible death of the Messiah was a part of the picture many Jews at the time had of the Messiah. Of course, the temporary triumph of evil could not result in the ultimate frustration of God's will. In the second parable, the owner of the vineyard would also have been seen as God, the vineyard as Israel, and the tenants as those who occupied any position of authority in Israel. The hearers would have moved from a natural horror at the behaviour of the tenants to an awareness that perhaps their own behaviour in relation to God was worthy of the condemnation they had so easily passed on the actors in the realistic story. The story in the Gospel of Thomas of the children or servants who have been entrusted with a field and claim it as their own when the true owners arrive is possibly a variant of the same parable (No. 90). They denude themselves of their tenancy by their false claim to ownership.

Similarly, the Great Supper would work on two levels (No. 45). In Matthew's version a king holds a wedding feast for his son and, when the invited guests do not come and even go so far as to kill some of his servants, he sends troops to destroy the murderers and to lay waste their city. In Luke the host is simply a man, and he does not take vengeance on those who do not accept his invitation. In both versions, the servants are sent to gather the poor to the feast. Again, the hearers

---

[10] Argued more fully, O'Neill (1997b), pp. 166-170.

would be aghast at the behaviour of those invited and full of praise for the invitation to the poor to share the meal. Then they would reflect that perhaps their own behaviour was like the behaviour of the churlish neighbours with respect to God's invitation to them to share the banquet in the Kingdom of Heaven. Matthew appended to this parable another parable about a guest who appeared at the wedding feast without a wedding garment (No. 46; cf. the parable of Rabbi Johanan b. Zakkai, *bShab* 153a). It hardly fits the earlier story, for the poor invited at the last moment could not be expected to be properly dressed. By itself, this parable is a simple story about someone who did not respect the host enough to dress correctly, which would have a spiritual meaning when transferred to ourselves and God's invitation to a feast, the marriage of the Lamb (Rev 19.7-9).

There are three separate parables about the behaviour of servants who are left in charge of the house while the owner is away (Nos. 50, 56, 64). In the first (No. 50), the good servants are contrasted with the wicked servants. The situation is common; the hearers would deplore the servants who began to beat their fellow servants and to eat and drink with the drunkards; and then they would begin to reflect on their own careless ways, behaving as though they might not be held accountable by God at any moment. Mark has a much shorter version of the same parable about the servants left with their tasks while the master is on a far journey (No. 56). Luke's version is about a master who was away at a wedding feast, which would have lasted for several days (No. 64). It praises the servants who are ready for his return, and tells how the master rewards them by making them sit at table and waiting on them himself.

The wise and foolish virgins (No. 51) were waiting for the bridegroom and the bride, not knowing how long the negotiations over the gifts for the bride's relatives would take.[11] The wise had reserves of oil for their lamps; the foolish none. By the time the foolish had gone to buy some more oil, the bridegroom had been lighted to the bride's house to bring her lighted to his father's house for the wedding and the wedding feast, and the doors were shut. The virgins—some wise, some foolish—were probably neighbours' children whose prudence and lack of foresight led to their inclusion in or exclusion from the

---

[11] Jeremias (1947; Eng. trans., 1963), pp. 171-174. The words *and the bride* (D family 1, all Latin versions, Syriac including Syriac Sinaiticus, Armenian) were probably omitted by scribes who thought the reference to the bride would distract from the allegory whereby the wise virgins represented the church. See Burkitt (1903), p. 4991.

feast.[12] Again, a realistic story which the hearers would enter into with glee, until they reflected that perhaps they would be like the foolish virgins should the bridegroom, the Messiah, come when they were not ready to escort him with their bright lamps. Similarly, the Parable of the Talents contrasts the enterprise of the servants who put to work the money the master had left in their charge with the timidity and lack of moral courage of the servant who in fear buried the talent so that he could be certain not to have lost it by foolish speculation (No. 52). The seed growing secretly (No. 54) similarly draws attention to the perfectly natural confidence of the farmer that good seed sown into well-prepared soil will grow a rich crop in the hope that the hearers will apply the same lesson to their own moral lives. The little parable of the two debtors (No. 59) contrasts the debtor who owes the equivalent of five hundred days' pay with a debtor who owes the equivalent of fifty days' pay. Both sue for the cancellation of their debt. The prayer of both is granted. Who will be the more grateful? Of course the hearers could hardly fail to think of the mercy of God to sinners.

In the parable of the Good Samaritan (No. 60) the priest and the Levite who saw the man left half-dead on the Jerusalem-Jericho road and passed by on the other side had probably just fulfilled their prescribed days of Temple service in Jerusalem and were hurrying home to their families. There was no religious reason for their failure to help, for, even if the man were dead, they would have had a duty to bury him (*mNaz* 7.1) Any impurity they incurred could easily be removed (Lev 22.3-7).[13] The Samaritan, who worshipped at the wrong Temple, showed he had a better grasp of what God required of him. This is another example of Jesus' teaching that obedience to God's moral laws

---

[12] Burkitt (1929).

[13] Bauckham tries to argue that the Love Commandment was an integral part of the parable and then concludes that Jesus was advancing a new idea, that the love commandment always overrides other commandments in case of conflict. In fact, there was at issue here no religious duty that cut across the plain moral duty laid down in the law. Bauckham's article (1998) is a good example of the prevalent notion that Jesus taught a higher law than the Law of Moses. Jesus was a teacher of the Law of Moses; see O'Neill (1980a), chapter 3. Barth similarly avoided the obvious meaning of the parable by running together the question, "Who is my neighbour?" with the story, so getting the result that the Samaritan was the type of Jesus; Jesus was not teaching that we should behave like the Samaritan but that we half-dead sinners should love him, even though he stands before us in the form of someone to be hated, as the lawyer believed he should hate a Samaritan. Barth (1938) KD I/2, pp. 460-462; CD I/2, pp. 417-419.

is the real test, not religious profession, however important religious profession may be (cf. No. 42).

The common title of the Parable of the Rich Fool (No. 63) captures the message. It is easy for us to be prudent about our possessions and forgetful of the fact that we must die.

Another admirable character in the parables is the servant who asked the owner of the land on which grew the fig tree that had failed to fruit for three years for one more year to dig it and dung it in the hope of making it productive (No. 65). If that treatment failed, then the tree should indeed be cut down. The hearers would understand that perhaps they were morally unproductive and had only been given time to do better by the intercession of a patient worker in the vineyard.

The woman who had ten coins and lost one (No. 70) is like the shepherd who had a hundred sheep and lost one (No. 39). I wonder if the hearers might not have reflected that the sorrow of the woman over the lost coin was rather unlike their own lack of concern about the one commandment of the ten that they failed to keep. Certainly the parable of the Prodigal Son (No. 71) is comfort for those who have run through all the rich gifts God has given them. The sensible thought in the mind of the Prodigal that he could not be worse off in his father's house as a servant would give fresh hope to any sinner who heard the story. And there was a message for those who felt like the elder brother. The unjust steward (No. 72) is another comforting story for sinners. The steward saw that, if only he were prepared to cancel his own cut of the transactions he had made on behalf of his master, he might be welcomed into other households as a steward when he lost his first position.[14] There was something he could do. The parable of the rich man—Dives—and Lazarus (No. 73) is a traditional story of great antiquity. Note the specific endorsement by Abraham of the Law of Moses, when Dives petitions that someone go from the dead and warn his still-living brothers: "If they hear not Moses and the prophets, neither will they be persuaded, though one rose from the dead." The Importunate Widow is a persistent woman who pesters a reluctant judge into giving her justice (No. 75). The hearers might well reflect that God is more ready to give than we to ask (Ps 86.5). The Pharisee in the Temple confessed the sins of the tax-collector (the Publican), and the Publican confessed his own sins (No. 76); it was the Publican who went home justified.

---

[14] Agnes Smith Lewis (1913), p. 116.

The two parables about a shepherd that are used in John's Gospel to open the chapter that is the tenth in our edition of the Gospel were probably once separate parables. The contrast between the shepherd, who comes by the door of the sheepfold, and the robber, who comes over the wall (No. 82) perhaps was originally a warning about disregarding the commandments of the law, which were given by God as a sort of fence and protection to his people (cf. Isa 5.2). The parable about the doorkeeper who recognizes the voice of the shepherd who knows the sheep by name and the sheep who also know the shepherd's voice (No. 83) was perhaps originally a hit at those who thought that the very popularity of a prophet was a sign of his being a false prophet; on the contrary, the doorkeeper opens to him and the sheep know to follow him.

The first of the two parables in the Gospel of Thomas that hold up to us pictures of admirable and not-so-admirable people, the parable of the wise fisherman and the great good fish (No. 89), is very like the parables of the Treasure, the Pearl and the Dragnet (Nos. 32, 33, 34). The woman who carried a jar of meal a long distance without realizing that the handle had broken and there was a hole in the jar so that she reached home only to find the jar empty (No. 91) is a parable meant at first to arouse sympathy. On reflection, she should have been more alert—and doesn't that apply also to our moral lives?

You wouldn't do that, would you?

Jesus told a large number of parables which explicitly or explicitly posed his hearers with a choice where the correct decision was pretty obvious (Class B in the Table of the Parables). He meant his hearers to see the connection between the prudent choices they made in everyday life and the similarly prudent choices they so often failed to make in their moral life.

No one would light a lamp and put it under a bushel, would they? (No. 5) Why, then, do we study God's Law and fail to use it to illuminate our way? You agree with your adversary on the way to court, don't you, if you know you are going to lose? (No. 7) Why don't we do the same with the good Lord before the day of judgment? No one can hope to serve two masters, can they? (No. 10) Why do we try to do so in our moral life? You don't give what is holy to the dogs or cast pearls before swine, do you? (No. 11) Why do we throw away our precious moral virtues with such abandon? If your son asks for bread, you don't give him a stone, do you? Or if he asks for a fish, a serpent? (No. 12) Do we follow the same principles in our moral education of our children? Do you gather grapes of thorns, or figs of thistles? (No. 15) Why do we expect to produce spiritual fruit if we pay no attention to the sort of people we are? You don't put a new patch on an old garment, do you? Nor do you put new wine into old wineskins (Nos. 19, 20). Similarly, for our old moral dilemmas we need the old commandments, and for the new moral challenge (like the man left half-dead by the roadside) we need new and imaginative ways of acting. You don't try to rob the strong man without first tying him up, do you? (No. 26) I suppose the devil would follow the same tactics in trying to get us to surrender to him all we most value. If a blind man leads a blind man, won't they both fall into the ditch? (No. 37) Why then do we so easily surrender the direction of our lives into the care of people who are as blind as we are? You would get up and give your friend food for his unexpected guest even though it was late and the whole household was in bed, wouldn't you? (No. 61) Why, then, do we hesitate to ask God for help in our need? Your wouldn't build a tower without counting the cost, or go to war without calculating the chances of victory, would you? (Nos. 68, 69) Do we apply the same prudence to the construction of our moral lives? The story of the assassin who tests his sword first (No. 92) is rather similar. You wouldn't expect your master, when you both came in from work on the farm, to ask you to sit down to a meal and wait on you, would you? (No. 74) Why do we think that one moral victory deserves a holiday from morality?

The metaphors

Jesus' teaching was very frequently pictorial. The moral life is like salt which, as taken from marshes along the shore, would have been mixed with other substances so that the pile of marsh salt could easily have lost its savour "through physical disintegration" (No. 2).[15] Just as Jerusalem was built on the hill of obedience, Mount Moriah, so that it would be impregnable and not hidden from the favour of the Lord (Psalm 38.9: my groaning is not hid), should not your life be built on the same hill? (No. 4) The good deeds of the moral life are compared to a lamp that shines and makes others thankful (No. 6). The body is like a house dependent on the light that comes through the window, the eye (No. 8). What do you fix your eye on, morally speaking?

---

[15] Deatrick (1962), pp. 43-44.

Your conscience is like a light within you (No. 9). What darkness, if the light that is within you is darkness. (The same metaphor seems to be used in Luke 11.36, but the meaning is almost impossible to discover and the text is corrupt [No. 62]). The entrance to the Kingdom of God is small and the way narrow; the entrance to destruction is wide and the way broad (No. 13). False prophets are like wolves in sheep's clothing (No. 14). As the sick need a physician, so sinners need a teacher in a way those who are well don't (No. 17). The sons of the bridechamber cannot fast while the bridegroom is present; they will fast when the bridegroom is forcibly taken away from them (No. 18). This was originally John the Baptist's answer to the question as to why Jesus' disciples did not have the special extra fast days observed by his own disciples and the Pharisees. John the Baptist used the well-known image of the Messiah as the bridegroom, an image from the Song of Solomon.[16] Just as a servant is not over his master, neither is a disciple over his teacher nor a messenger over him who sent him (No. 21).

A true prophet is not like a reed shaken by the wind (No. 22a). A kingdom divided against itself will be laid waste; a city or a house divided cannot stand (Nos. 24, 25). Someone delivered from a great evil obsession is like a haunted house that is rid of a demon, who will easily return with more mates if nothing is put in his place (No. 27). What is eaten can at worst temporarily defile; what comes out of the mouth is much more serious (No. 36). The idea that Jesus was abolishing the Jewish food regulations is already found in the patent marginal gloss of Mark 7.19. This interpretation rested on a misunderstanding of the Semitic relative negative by which the less important matter is negated in order to draw attention to the prime importance of the other term.[17] At their worst, Jews regarded Gentiles as dogs and Gentiles regarded Jews as dogs. Jesus twitted the Gentile woman who came to ask him to heal her daughter with the worst Jewish version of the comparison, which she was willing to accept if only the child could be healed (No. 38). The application of the proverbial saying that, where the corpse is, there the vultures will gather is hard to discover (No. 47; cf. Job 39.27-30). As the budding of the fig tree presages harvest, so repentance gives promise of the coming of the Kingdom (No. 48). The Son of Man will divide the nations as a shepherd separates the sheep from the goats (No. 53). It is not clear what the metaphor of being salted with fire means; somehow the fire purifies without destroying (No. 55). Any teacher could be compared to a physician who

---

[16] O'Neill (1988).
[17] O'Neill (1995), p. 150 and n. 34.

cannot heal himself (No. 57). Any teaching could be compared to wine; and who would prefer new wine to old? (No. 58) The Messiah will be like a steward at a feast who refuses entry to those who claim acquaintance but have done harm to his house (No. 66).

John's Gospel contains a number of metaphors not found in the Synoptic Gospels. Their application is not always easy to discover. The Spirit is like wind; you don't know where it comes from and where it goes (No. 77). John the Baptist compares himself to the friend of the bridegroom (No. 78). The prophet and the Messiah are compared to sower and reaper (No. 79). A servant can be dismissed; a son not (No. 80). Work while it is day; night comes when no work can be done. You do not stumble in daylight, but stumble easily at night (Nos. 81, 82, 86). If a grain does not die—and *die* must mean *transform itself into something else*—it produces no harvest (No. 85). The Messiah is like a vine, the disciples like branches, and the Father like a vine-dresser (No. 87). A woman forgets her birth pangs in the joy of bearing a child (No. 88).

It is natural to find that the metaphors are elusive since they have a proverbial quality, which fits them for use in many different circumstances. They are memorable and likely to be preserved by the tradition in instances where their use was lost. The parables that hold up for our admiration good characters and for our condemnation evil characters (Class A) are much easier to read. So, too, are the instances of prudent choices we all make in everyday life (Class B) easy to translate and to apply to our moral lives. But wherever the point of the metaphors in Class C is clear, it conforms to the pattern already discerned in the other two classes. Taken as whole, the parables in Class A and Class B and Class C all make sense on a moral plane. The perfectly understandable desire of commentators to turn our attention from the story to the one who told the story has led to an overemphasis on the centrality of decision in the stories. Unfortunately it has often also led to attempts to make the stories into attacks by Jesus on the law as such, as though there were a higher morality, one rooted in allegiance to him, above the moral commands of God the Father in the Law of Moses. The ironic effect has been to turn a great corpus of teaching which emphasized above all the necessity of doing God's revealed will into stories that simply called for allegiance to the Messiah. The Messiah was portrayed as a teacher who taught a morality above ordinary morality, surely an impossibly anachronistic picture. Not only anachronistic but immoral.

THE PARABLES OF JESUS

		Matthew	Mark	Luke	Thomas	John	Class
1.	You are salt	5.13a					C
2.	Salt that has lost its savour	5.13b	9.50b	14.34-5			C
3.	Light	5.14					C
4.	City on hill	5.14			32		C
5.	Lamp	5.15	4.21	8.16;11.33	33		B
6.	Let your light shine	5.16					C
7.	Going before judge	5.25-6		12.58-9			B
8.	Body's light	6.22-23a		11.34	24		C
9.	If the light within you is darkness	6.23b					C
10.	No man can serve two masters	6.24		6.13	47		B
11.	Holy things to dogs; pearls before swine	7.6			93		B
12.	The son's requests	7.9-11		11.11-13			B
13.	Narrow door	7.13-14		13.24			C
14.	Wolves in sheep's clothing	7.15					C
15.	By their fruits	7.16-20; 12.33-37		6.43-45	45		B
16.	House built upon the rock	7.24-27		6.47-49			A
17.	Physician and the sick	9.12-13	2.17	5.31-32			C
18.	Sons of the bridechamber	9.14-15	2.18-20	5.33-35 104			C
19.	Patch	9.16	2.21	5.36	47		B

		Matthew	Mark	Luke	Thomas	John	Class
20.	Wineskins	9.17	2.22	5.37-38	47		B
21.	Disciple and teacher	10.24		6.40		13.16	C
22.	Nothing is hidden	10.26-27	4.22	12.2-3; 8.17			C
22a.	Reed shaken by the wind	11.7		7.24			C
23.	Children in the marketplace	11.16-19		7.31-35			A
24.	Divided kingdom	12.25a	3.24-25	11.17a			C
25.	Divided house (city)	12.25b	3.25	11.17b			C
26.	Strong man spoiled	12.29	3.27	11.21-22	35		B
27.	Return of the unclean spirit	12.43-45		11.24-26			C
28.	Sower	13.3-8	4.3-8	8.5-8	9		A
29.	Wheat and tares	13.24-30			57		A
30.	Mustard seed	13.31-32	4.30-32	13.18-19	20		A
31.	Leaven	13.33		13.20-21	96		A
32.	Treasure	13.44			109		A
33.	Pearl	13.45-46			76		A
34.	Dragnet	13.47-48					A
35.	Householder and his store	13.52					A
36.	True defilement	15.10-11, 15-20	7.14-23		14		C
37.	Blind guide	15.14		6.39	34		B
38.	Children and dogs	15.26-27	7.27-28				C
39.	Lost sheep	18.12-14		15.4-7	107		A
40.	Ungrateful servant	18.23-35					A

		Matthew	Mark	Luke	Thomas	John	Class
41.	Labourers in vineyard	20.1-16					A
42.	Two sons	21.28-32					A
43.	Wicked tenants and the son	21.37-39	12.1-5a, 6-8	20.9-15a	65		A
44.	Wicked tenants and the owner's return	21.33-36, 40-41	12.1,5b, 9	20.15b			A
45.	Great supper	22.1-10		14.16-24	64		A
46.	Guest without a wedding garment	22.11-14					B
47.	Vultures and corpse	24.28		17.37			C
48.	Budding fig tree	24.32-33	13.28-29	21.29-31			C
49.	Thief in the night	24.43-44		12.39-40	21; 103		B
50.	Faithful and unfaithful servants	24.45-51		12.42-46			A
51.	Wise and foolish virgins	25.1-13					A
52.	Talents	25.14-30		19.12-27			A
53.	Sheep and goats	25.31-46					C
54.	Seed growing secretly		4.26-29				A
55.	Salted with fire		9.49				C
56.	Doorkeeper cf. 64		13.33-37				A
57.	Physician, heal thyself			4.23			C
58.	Old wine and new			5.39	47		C
59.	Two debtors			7.41-43			A
60.	Good Samaritan			10.25-37			A
61.	Friend at midnight			11.5-8			B
62.	If your whole body is light			11.36	24		C

		Matthew	Mark	Luke	Thomas	John	Class
63.	Rich fool			12.16-21	63		A
64.	Waiting servants cf. 56			12.35-38			A
65.	Barren fig tree			13.6-9			A
66.	Closed door	(7.22-23; 25.10-11)		13.24-30			C
67.	Choice of places at table			14.7-11			B
68.	Counting the cost: tower			14.28-30			B
69.	Counting the cost: campaign cf. 92			14.31-32			B
70.	Lost coin			15.8-10			A
71.	Prodigal son			15.11-32			A
72.	Unjust steward			16.1-8			A
73.	Rich man and Lazarus			16.19-31			B
74.	Unprofitable servant			17.7-10			A
75.	Importunate widow			18.1-8			A
76.	Pharisee and Publican			18.9-14			A
77.	Wind blows where it will					3.8	C
78.	Friend of the bridegroom cf. 18					3.29	C
79.	Sower and reaper					4.36-37	C
80.	Slave and son					8.35	C
81.	Night comes when no one can work					9.4	C
82.	Shepherd and robber					10.1-2	A
83.	Shepherd, gatekeeper and sheep					10.3-5	A
84.	Are there not twelve hours in a day?					11.9-10	C
85.	Grain of wheat					12.24	C

	Matthew	Mark	Luke	Thomas	John	Class
86. Walk while you have light					12.35-36	C
87. Vine					15.1-8	C
88. Woman's birthpangs					16.21	C
89. Wise fisherman and great good fish cf. 32, 33, 34				8		A
90. Little children living in field not theirs				21		C
91. Woman who lost the meal without knowing it				97		A
92. Assassin tests sword before using it cf. 68, 69				98		B

Class A: Stories about admirable people—and not-so-admirable people.
Class B: Situations of choice, in which one choice is obviously better than another.
Class C: Metaphors.

6

The Events around the Birth and Resurrection

Dennis Nineham, in 1981 Warden of Keble, Oxford, once said to a visiting lecturer in conversation over a cup of coffee, "If it were discovered that Jesus was evil, it would destroy my Christian faith. If it were discovered that Jesus didn't exist, it would make no difference to my faith." I agree with the first statement, and reports that Jesus cursed a fig tree for not bearing fruit when it was not the season for figs (Mark 11.13), for example, do raise questions about his goodness.[1] Such slurs have to be answered, or no one can easily follow Jesus. The second statement is interesting. Like the first statement, it presupposes that historians can arrive at very probable conclusions about events in the distant past, even when those events have been predominantly reported by partisan observers, many of whom wrote long after the event. We can raise and answer, with some confidence, questions such as, Did Jesus exist? We can also raise and answer, with some confidence, questions such as, Was Joseph Jesus' father?; Why did Joseph and Mary go to Bethlehem for the birth of Jesus?; Did Paul think that the tomb of Jesus was empty?; and Was the tomb empty?

The answers to those questions will not, by themselves, create faith; nor will the answers to those questions, by themselves, destroy faith. But surely they will make some difference to people who are wondering whether to attach their allegiance to Jesus or whether to withdraw their allegiance from Jesus. Nineham concedes that some sorts of historical knowledge—knowledge about Jesus' moral character—affect his faith. Why does he not concede that other sorts of historical knowledge—such as knowledge about whether Jesus existed

---

[1] The symbolic incident originally circulated as a separate story, without being set at any particular time of the year. When a collector of stories set the incident at Passover, an acute scribe noticed that no fig tree was likely to bear figs then and inserted the note. The symbolic cursing would have had no point unless it were the time for figs.

or did not exist—affect his faith? G.A. Wells, in a notable modern attempt to show that Jesus did not exist, ended with these words.

> Finally, will the thesis that Jesus did not exist—if it comes to be accepted—have much effect on Christianity? I think not, if theologians play their hand carefully. "I believe in God the Father Almighty" has already been revised by John Robinson to something like "I believe in Ultimate Reality". To reinterpret the further phrase "and in Jesus Christ his only Son, our Lord" should not present insuperable difficulty. We shall, perhaps, be told that belief in Jesus is not at all the same thing as believing that he lived 1,950 years ago. Theologians have indicated that they are ready to apply their ingenuity to the problem, should the need arise. ... To prevent people from seeing the sunlight, one can place them in a dungeon. When this becomes impracticable, the same result can be achieved by creating a universal fog...[2]

I do not wish to make extravagant claims about the effect that historical conclusions may have on anyone's faith. I have sympathy with the friend who once said to me that he could not base anything so important as religious belief on reports that Jesus rose from the dead. But historical conclusions must have some effect, and do have some effect. This chapter will be devoted to discussing the reliability of a few reports about the events surrounding Jesus' birth and alleged resurrection.

Was Joseph Jesus' natural father?

It is commonly argued that interest in the birth of Jesus is a late development in Christian doctrine; that Jesus was first thought to be made Messiah at the crucifixion, then regarded as Messiah during his earthly ministry and made Messiah at his baptism by John, then regarded as Messiah at his miraculous birth of a virgin, and finally regarded as Messiah or Son of God from all eternity. On this account, interest in the circumstances of Jesus' conception and birth would be a late interest. Paul and Mark are said to have no knowledge of the alleged virgin birth.

This story is largely based on a misunderstanding of the force of the word *made* in Acts 2.36: "Let all the house of Israel know for sure that God has made both Lord and Christ this Jesus whom you crucified." The verb *made* does not, in Hebrew usage, mean that God decided to turn Jesus, who had not previously been Lord or Christ, into some-

---

[2] Wells (1975), pp.206-207; 2nd revised ed. (1986), pp. 216-217.

one who was to be honoured as Lord and Messiah. Rather it means that God enthroned as Lord and Christ the one who had always been that (cf. 2 Kings 17.29-33; John 6.15).[3] Jewish expectation was that the Messiah would remain hidden, and would have to suffer just like his father David, before God revealed his glory and enthroned him in the sight of Israel and the Gentiles.

Interest in Jesus' birth would be alive right from the moment when people began to wonder whether or not he was the Messiah. Mark's Gospel reports the crowds at Nazareth as scoffing at the messianic pretensions he seemed to be showing by his public preaching. "Is not this the carpenter, the son of Mary, and brother of James and Justus and Jude and Simon? And are not his brothers here with us?" (Mark 6.3)

Paul probably cites an early creed about Jesus in Rom 1.3-4:

> That which was promised beforehand
> through his prophets
> in the holy scriptures
> concerning his Son:
> born of the seed of David
> according to the flesh;
> marked out with power as Son of God
> according to the Spirit of Holiness;
> from the resurrection from the dead
> Jesus Christ our Lord.

This creed, if I have divided it correctly, is interested in the double origin of Jesus, legally the son of David through his purported father, Joseph, and also the result of the direct work of the Holy Spirit. The genealogies of Jesus in Matt 1.1-17 and Luke 3.23-38 trace his Davidic descent through Joseph, and have often been taken as showing ignorance of the story that he was virginally conceived. Not so. Joseph in law was his father, and Jesus was a son of David because Joseph was. Even the reading of Matt 1.16 in the Syriac palimpsest of the Gospels found at St Catherine's monastery at Mount Sinai, "Joseph, to whom being betrothed Mary the Virgin, begat Jesus, who is called the Christ," was not thought to contradict the story. These are the terms in which Jesus' birth would have been recorded in the family records.[4]

---

[3] For a fuller discussion, see O'Neill (1995), chapter 1.
[4] Lewis (1910), xiv-xvi; (1913), chapter 3.

It is often said that the story of the virginal conception of Jesus was made up long after the event by a misreading of Isa 7.14, which in older translations and in the LXX, a Greek translation of the Hebrew original, reads, "Behold, a virgin shall conceive, and bear a son, and shall call his name Immanuel," but in most modern translations something like, "Look, the young woman is with child and shall bear a son, and shall name him Immanuel" (New Revised Standard Version). This is in a passage where Isaiah tells King Ahaz that the Lord will give him a hopeful sign. The older translators are likely to be right. The promised sign has to be something surprising, and Isaiah's own wife being going to have a child is not likely to have been particularly notable. The interpretation that suggests that the young woman is already pregnant is not expressly stated in the Hebrew and is unlikely. The word the older translations and the LXX took to mean *virgin* does naturally mean that, and Prov 30.19 and Song of Solomon 6.8 scarcely prove the opposite.

In any case, even if the LXX be an inaccurate translation, it is evidence of an early understanding of the passage. This is confirmed by the *Testament of Joseph* 20.2, 8-12, which gives the content of a vision. From Judah was begotten a virgin and from her was begotten a spotless lamb. The lamb was also like a lion. He conquered the beasts that attacked him. Because of him angels and men and all the earth rejoiced. This account seems to have been written before Jesus was born.[5]

It is unlikely that the prophecy produced the story. Rather, the circumstances of Jesus' conception would be taken as signs that he was the promised one—or that he was an impostor. The slur on Jesus' birth, that he was not Joseph's natural son, was not only hinted at in Mark 6.3, but was stated in John 8.41,48: "*We* are not born of fornication. Do we not rightly say of you that you are a Samaritan and have a demon?"

The charge that Jesus was the son of a soldier, named as Pantera in some early sources, probably stems from the first century. Origen in his refutation of the philosopher Celsus' attacks on Christianity cites a report that Celsus claimed to have known a Jew who had a conversation with Jesus in which the Jew charged Jesus with making up the story of the virginal conception and that his mother Mary was driven away by her husband, a carpenter, on the charge of adultery (*Contra*

---

[5] O'Neill (1979).

Celsum 1.28).⁶ Tertullian seems to be alluding to Jewish attacks on Jesus as the son of the carpenter or of a harlot (*de Spectaculis* 30.5-6).⁷

What is more likely, that followers of Jesus made up the story of the virginal conception of Jesus, so running the risk of the counter-charge that Jesus was conceived by someone other than Joseph, Mary's husband, or that Joseph did not conceive Jesus? It seems clear that Joseph was not the natural father of Jesus. Matt 1.18-25 is at least based on the fact that Mary was pregnant before she and Joseph had come together.

Why did Joseph and Mary go to Bethlehem for the birth of Jesus?

Herod the Great died in 4 BC. He was a client king in the Roman empire. At his death Augustus divided his kingdom between his heirs: Archelaus became ethnarch (above the rank of tetrarch, but below that of king) of Judaea, Idumaea and Samaria; Herod Antipas became tetrarch of Galilee and Peraea; and the mild man Philip became tetrarch of Trachonitis, Batanaea and Ituraea. Archelaus scandalized decent opinion and misgoverned his realm. He divorced his wife and married a woman who had been married to his half-brother, by whom she had had children. He built a city in his own honour and restored the palace at Jericho at vast expense. A deputation of Jewish and Samaritan aristocrats to Rome laid such serious charges against him that Augustus summoned him to Rome, dismissed him from office and banished him to Gaul. Judaea, Idumaea and Samaria were now put under a Roman governor of the equestrian order and attached to the province of Syria. Quirinius, a Roman senator, was governor of Syria, despatched by Augustus in AD 6-7 to his post with instructions to make an assessment of property at the same time as Coponius was sent to Judaea. Quirinius visited Judaea to assess Jewish property and to liquidate the estate of the exiled Archelaus. For the first time Judaea came under direct Roman rule, and the property census was the first taste of the loss of the buffer between them and the Romans that had previously been supplied by Herod and his heirs (Josephus, *Ant* 18.1-3).⁸

In Luke 2.1-5 we read an account of how Joseph and Mary left Nazareth and came to Bethlehem because of the census under Quirinius.

---

⁶ Translated by Chadwick (1953), p. 28.
⁷ See the full discussion in Horbury (1998b), pp. 176-179.
⁸ See the account in the new Schürer (1973), vol. 1, pp. 354-357.

There is little doubt that this is the census of AD 6. Luke also states that this census was the result of a decree by Augustus that all the world should be taxed. Augustus had held a universal census in 8 BC and a partial census, confined to Italy, in 4 BC. There was no universal census in AD 6, but T.P. Wiseman has pointed out that in AD 6 Augustus, having introduced a five percent inheritance tax, may well have asked provincial governors to provide an up-to-date list of wealthy Roman citizens resident in the provinces. If so, Luke's source could have conflated this demand, which applied only to Roman citizens, with the historically well-established demand for a census of the property of the subject peoples.[9] But that is the least of the difficulties in Luke's account.

Although itinerant workers had to return home during a census, there was no rule that required people to return to their ancestral home. An itinerant worker would not have to take his wife on a journey to be present at a census. If Joseph and Mary were living in Nazareth, they were in the area governed by the tetrarch Herod Antipas and would not have been subject to direct Roman taxation and so not required to register in the census in Judaea.

Nor is that all. According to Luke 1.5, John the Baptist was conceived in the reign of Herod king of Judaea, almost certainly Herod the Great, who died in 4 BC. Jesus was conceived shortly afterwards. And of course Matthew puts Jesus' birth during the reign of Herod. Luke also records that Jesus began his ministry in the fifteenth year of Tiberias Caesar, which would be between August AD 28 and August AD 29, when Jesus was about thirty years' old (Luke 31.23). So the story of the birth of Jesus in the year of the census does not fit the other chronological remarks in Luke's Gospel, let alone Matthew's.

The author of the Third Gospel was an historian working with older sources, as he tells us in his prologue, Luke 1.1-4. It seems likely that he has here combined two pretty accurate accounts of events in Bethlehem. One account tells of the census of Quirinius in AD 6-7 which outraged Jewish religious susceptibilities. This comprised Luke 2.1-3. It ended with the remark that anyone away from home had to return to his home town for the census. That remark led Luke to combine the account with Luke 2.4-7, the account of how Joseph, a son of David, took Mary to Bethlehem for the birth of the child.[10]

---

[9] Wiseman (1987), pp. 479-80.

[10] The word *to be enrolled* at the beginning of Luke 2.5 is not found in the first hand of the Codex Alexandrinus (A) or in the Syriac Peshitta or in Chrysippus and Eusebius.

Luke thought the two accounts were connected, but he had a further reason arising from his own theology. He was glad to show that Jesus was born in obedience to the decree of Caesar Augustus because Jesus was destined to be the child in whose name the Roman empire would eventually worship the one true God (for Acts 28.30-31 is a sort of prophecy of the amazing expansion of the church in the empire).

But if Joseph did not take Mary to Bethlehem for the purpose of the census, why did he want the child to be born away from home? The answer seems to be that he wanted the child to be born in David's city because he was a son of David and perhaps the child was the long-promised Messiah. This was to be in accordance with the prophecy in Micah 5.1-5: though Bethlehem was insignificant among the thousands of Judah, out of it would come for the Lord a ruler in Israel. When she who was in travail had brought forth, there would be a great home-coming of Israel. The Messiah would gather his people.

Did Paul think that the tomb of Jesus was empty?

Paul must have thought that the tomb was empty because he had been a Pharisee. What distinguished Pharisees from Sadducees was that the Pharisees believed that the soul was immortal and at the resurrection would pass into a pure and transformed body at the day of judgment while the Sadducees believed neither that the soul survived the body nor that there was to be a resurrection of the body (Acts 23.8; Josephus *War* 2.162-166; 3.374; *contra Apionem* 2.218; *Jewish Antiquities* 18.12-17). The term *resurrection* meant the transformation of the body. Since Paul used this term of Jesus, he meant that Jesus' body had been transformed ahead of the expected transformation of the bodies of all at the day of judgment.

Paul is sometimes held to deny this belief by the statement to be found in 1 Cor 15.50:

> And this, brothers, I say:
> Flesh and blood cannot inherit the kingdom of God,
> Nor does corruption inherit incorruption.

This is one saying in a long chain of sayings inserted into the copy of Paul's first epistle to the Corinthians at our 1 Cor 15.12-50, but there is no reason to doubt that Paul would have agreed with the tenor of the catena. The saying is a warning to put off corruption in order to be ready for the coming of the kingdom of God which none could enter unless purified by grace from their sins. The term *flesh and blood* in the first statement of the moral couplet does not mean that the human body as such cannot enter the kingdom but that the human body marred and stained by sin and unpurified by grace could not enter the kingdom of God.

In 1 Cor 15.1-8 Paul cites a creed and concludes by putting Christ's appearance to him, some time after the other appearances, at the end. The fact that Paul's appearance was in a vision from heaven has led scholars to conclude that Paul thought of the other appearances as purely visionary, not entailing the resurrection of Jesus' body. I have already given one argument that makes this conclusion unlikely; that is, Paul would not have described Jesus as risen from the dead unless he had meant risen in a transformed body. Paul knew the story of Saul and the witch of Endor, as well as many other stories of the dead appearing in visions to the living like the story of Jeremiah's appearance to Onias, who had been high priest and who prayed for his people before they went into battle under Judas Maccabaeus (2 Macc 15.12-16). If he held that Jesus' appearance to him was of that nature, he would not have said that Jesus was risen from the dead.

When we turn to the substance of the creed in 1 Cor 15.3b-4, this conclusion is strengthened. It is said that Christ died, Christ was buried, Christ was raised on the third day, and Christ appeared to Cephas and then to the Twelve. If Paul held that the body of Jesus was still buried somewhere in the Holy Land, he would have said merely, "Christ died and Christ appeared to Cephas and then to the Twelve." The three terms *died, was buried* and *is raised* go together and entail the usual Jewish belief in the bodily resurrection.[11]

Was the tomb empty?

Gerd Lüdemann in a thorough and passionate book on the resurrection argues that the appearances of Jesus and the resultant proclamation that he had risen produced the narrative of the tomb discovered empty by the women: "on the basis of the kerygma an apologetic legend developed with women as recipients of the proclamation of the resurrection at the place where Jesus was buried."[12]

---

[11] See, for example, the arguments of W.K. Lowther Clarke (1929), pp. 102-107.
[12] Lüdemann (1994), English trans. p. 118.

The difficulty with this explanation is that none of the recipients of visions of Jesus after his death would have concluded that he had been raised from the dead unless there had been reports of the empty tomb. The extraordinary story in Matthew's Gospel that, at the crucifixion, an earthquake occurred, the tombs were opened and many bodies of the saints who had fallen asleep were raised, leaving their tombs and going into the holy city (Matt 27.52-53), which brings with it all sorts of problems, at least shows that no one was likely to turn visionary appearances into resurrection narratives without some evidence of empty tombs. And any who challenged the proclamation of the resurrection of Jesus would only have had to produce a plausible body of Jesus in order to refute the claim that he had risen. Those Jews who did not accept the claims made about Jesus regularly provided other explanations as to how the tomb came to be empty, explanations such that the disciples stole the body or that a pious Jew, a gardener, hid the body in a well, perhaps with the idea of giving it honourable burial later.[13]

The disciples of Jesus most likely fled from Jerusalem and returned to Galilee. There is a strong tradition that Jesus was buried by a pious Jew or Jews who were not immediate followers; witness the artless statement in Acts 13.27-29: "For they that dwell in Jerusalem and their rulers ... desired Pilate that he should be slain. And when they had fulfilled all that was written of him, they took him down from the tree and laid him in a sepulchre" (cf. Matt 27.57-60; Mark 15.42-46; Luke 23.5--55; John 19.38-42). In Luke's version of the discovery of the empty tomb by women, the women are not the variously named immediate followers of Jesus in the other accounts, but an anonymous group, only identified as immediate followers in an appendix at the end of the story (Luke 23.50-24.9, with the appendix, 24.10). It looks as though the names of women and their identification with followers of Jesus came later. The two men who went to the tomb in the account in John's Gospel were arguably pious men, not disciples of Jesus, who went to the tomb to honour the dead prophet. Only later are these two men turned into Peter and the Beloved Disciple. The text of John 20.8-9, preserved in the supplement to the Codex Bezae, shows the true nature of the original account: "Then the other disciple also entered—he was the one who had arrived first—and he saw and did *not* believe, for they did not yet know the scripture that it was

---

[13] For details see Horbury (1998b), pp. 176-179.

necessary for him to rise from the dead."[14] The empty tomb by itself did not produce belief (and still does not); it has to be put together with much else.

Clearly anyone who did not believe in God and who does not believe that God can raise the dead would give a moment's credence to any of the evidence about Jesus' birth or death that I have been exploring. Such a person would conclude that there must be other explanations: if Joseph was not the natural father of Jesus, some other man must have been; if the tomb was actually empty, someone must have moved the body, for good reasons or bad. It is also true that people can be believing Christians who think that supernatural events are not required for belief. My simple purpose has been to show that there were grounds in the events for the traditional beliefs.

Human beings are condemned (if that is the right word) to basing all their most fundamental beliefs and all their most important decisions on incomplete evidence and hints rather than on complete proof. God no doubt wants the clever and persevering people who would write and read books like this to acknowledge his power and glory, but he is obviously not going to make it easy for them. He may even show himself more clearly to others than the clever and sophisticated. Once we catch a glimpse of how fantastic it is that we can think at all, and realize the inescapable mystery of the explicability of the universe, we shall begin to be filled with the awe that is the true ground of worship. Then we won't be surprised at how surprising events often turn out to be.

---

[14] O'Neill (1997a), p. 85.

7

Why is the New Testament Doctrine of the Death of Christ So Elusive?

Nowhere in the New Testament do we find anyone wrestling with the doctrine of the atonement. Every writer simply assumes that sinners are reconciled to God, that atonement is made, by the death of Christ on the cross. No writer ever stops to explain how Christ's death atones. If we are ever given a glimpse of the mechanism of atonement, the glimpse is so brief that we cannot be sure that we have seen aright; ἱλαστήριον (*hilasterion*) flashes before our eyes, but what does ἱλαστήριον mean? Jesus himself only once is reported to have used a technical term about his death, when he spoke of the Son of man's giving his life a ransom for many (Matt 20.28; Mark 10.45). A precious hint, perhaps; but not so much an explanation as an allusion to what everyone knows. And perhaps even this one word promises too much; I am pretty sure we should accept as original the reading of the Washington Codex at Mark 10.45 and take the word to be *washing* instead of *ransom*, λούτρον instead of λύτρον: Jesus said the Son of man was to give his life to wash away the sins of many. If I am right, a high-sounding term like "redemption", which seems to promise a theory, has become a homely image of a servant waiting at table and washing the feet of the invited guests; not theory, but an action with consequences. The death of a man is service and cleansing.

The only other place where Jesus might be thought to teach about the atonement is in the words over the bread and the cup at the Last Supper. Clearly, any theory of the atonement will have to make sense of what was said and done in the Upper Room, of what happened at Calvary, and of what happens when Christians gather for the Lord's Supper. The words may betray a theory or a number of theories, but they do not stop to teach any theory.

There are even large tracts of the New Testament which seem to avoid any theorizing about the death of Christ. In the Acts of the

Apostles no one is ever made to say more than that Christ had to die for the forgiveness of sins: δεῖ, it was necessary that the Messiah had to suffer. When Isaiah 53 is cited in Acts 8, the citation takes in no verse that might suggest a theory (Isa 53.7-8 in Acts 8.32-33).

However, in the epistles of the New Testament and in Revelation we have a good number of passages that offer us images to work on, and images are suggestive of structures; and structures we are able to explore. The trouble is that either the images and the structures they reveal still leave us clueless about the actual mechanism of the atonement, or they suggest a mechanism of the atonement that conflicts with clear principles actually stated in the Bible. The images which the New Testament offers us either still leave us guessing about how the atonement was meant to work, or they give us an atonement that flies in the face of explicit Biblical teaching.

It is said often enough that Christ redeemed us or ransomed us by dying on the cross (1 Tim 2.6, if not Matt 20.28; Mark 10.45). Redemption, ἀπολύτρωσις, and its cognates is very common: Rom 3.24; 8.23; 1 Cor 1.30; Col 1.14; Eph 1.7, 14; 4.30; Heb 9.12, 15; 11.35; 1 Peter 1.18. Perhaps the term refers to sinners as slaves who are manumitted and made adopted sons (Rom 8.14, 15; Gal 3.26; 4.5-7; 5.1; 1 Cor 7.23). Or perhaps the term refers to sinners who were prisoners of war, freed when the enemy was defeated (Heb 2.14, 15; 1 Cor 15.55; Rev 12.10; 2 Tim 1.10). The trouble is that these images of the manumission of slaves or the freeing of captives do not explain how Christ's death achieves the liberty. Perhaps the death of a testator makes the beneficiaries of the will heirs; that is true enough in our legal world, but why did this testator, Christ, have to die before we could get what he wants to give us? Perhaps our captors, the devil and his angels, were defeated by a trick, when they arranged the killing of Jesus and found to their discomfort that they had crucified the Lord of Glory (1 Cor 2.8); we can understand the strategy of ambush, but why did Christ adopt that strategy to defeat the enemy and free the prisoners? Why did he have to die in the successful ambush? We can imagine a victorious prince dying at the moment of victory, the victory that freed us, but why did he *have* to? Why could this enemy be defeated no other way?

The same set of questions arises when we look at the idea that atonement is the justification of sinners. Granted sinners are made righteous or are treated as righteous because they have faith in a crucified Lord, why is it that the one they have faith in had to die for them?

The Death of Christ

Perhaps the great Judge acquits the guilty because of their faith in the blood of the advocate; but why did this advocate have to die for his clients? Perhaps the death of the advocate represents a restitution of the Judge's outraged honour, or the payment of an enormous debt. This we could understand: the price of liberty is not only eternal vigilance; it may also be the readiness to sacrifice our young men and women in war.

The trouble with this line of thinking is that it runs up against two pieces of quite explicit Biblical teaching. The first is that no judge remains a just judge who acquits the guilty on payment of a price. That is explicitly stated in the Bible (Ex 23.7: οὐ δικαιώσεις τὸν ἀσεβῆ ἕνεκεν δώρων); but I would hazard a guess that the Biblical writers to a man would accept my extension of this principle: No judge remains a just judge who himself arranges to pay himself a price in order to appear to be just in acquitting the guilty.

The second Biblical fact is that sinners were forgiven by God before Christ died. The death of Christ was not always necessary, it seems, for the forgiveness of sins. If the judge could forgive sins without the death of his Son, why did his Son have to die? The explanation offered, that justice had to be satisfied by this death, does not seem always to have been the case—yet the explanation was supposed to show the necessity of the death.

Or let us turn to another picture of how sinners are reconciled to God through Christ. They are said to die with Christ (Rom 6.8) or even to be incorporated into Christ by dying with him (although that reading of the phrase ἐν Χριστῷ, in Christ, seems to me more than doubtful, as I shall argue in Chapter 8). The picture is clear enough and has a clear meaning when applied to our case. We need to "die" in the sense of putting to death all that separates us from God, our sinful passions and habits. But this is the stuff of all true morality and religion the world over. We need the *symbol* of death, but do we need the actual death of one who did not need the symbol himself? A sinner's struggles to mortify his flesh, struggles which perhaps ended in actual death, might inspire us to mortify our own passions, but why should the death of *Christ* do this for us? Christ was not a sinner who showed us how to struggle against sin even to the point of death. How does *his* death work?

Certainly it would show great love to die for those who were deserving, and even greater love to die for the undeserving (Rom 5.7, 8), but these two moral facts do not explain how the death of Christ was to the advantage of those he died for. We can see and understand the advantage accruing from the death of soldiers and civilians in a war: the death of the soldiers and their readiness to die is the necessary cause of the victory of one side; and both sides gain from the victory, the speedier and the less bloody the better. But how did Jesus' contemporaries, let alone the members of subsequent generations, belong to Jesus' "side" or his enemy's "side"? And in battle no *one* death is regarded as necessary. Why was Christ's death required? How did his death win others a victory?

A final way of explaining Christ's love and its effects is drawn from what we know about personal relationships. We know, or think we know, that all personal reconciliation involves the readiness of the innocent party to suffer. Just as the healing of a physical wound requires the expenditure of energy in the growth of new bones and tissue, so the healing of a wound between people involves the expenditure of energy in forbearance, willingness to rebuild, energy to re-create new bonds that are the new tissue of relationships.

This may all be true, but we are still not told why Christ had to die to make possible the specific output of energy necessary to repair the damaged relationships we are involved in. The only answer is, We must do what he did. But that is not quite satisfactory, even if it qualifies at all to be a doctrine of how Christ atones for our sins. It is not satisfactory because it still does not explain his *death*. What this image requires is that the healing and atoning party in the broken, wounded relationship should stay alive and suffer. Death must be avoided at all costs, because once the healing person dies, no more healing is possible. At best, the death of the healer might bring remorse to those left alive. Christ did not stay alive suffering to reconcile sinners to each other and to the Father; he died. Why?

But, it may be said, he rose again and still lives. We may both follow his example of self-giving love and join ourselves to him in following this pattern in order to restore the damaged tissue of the world. This image may explain how we have been the recipients of healing from Christ-like saviours, and may provide a model for how we may be Christ-like saviours of others. It does not obviously or clearly explain why Jesus of Nazareth two thousand years ago had to die for us.

Whichever way we turn we get no answer to our question, Why did Christ die for sinners?—or we get answers that seem to contradict the rest of scripture. We are told he died to redeem slaves and captives, to justify the ungodly, to enable sinners to die to sin, and to show his love for sinners, but no New Testament writer stops to explain the mechanics of the deal.

The image of sacrifice

You will notice that I have left one very prominent image aside; I have talked very little of the image which perhaps lies behind all the fragmentary pictures I have hitherto mentioned. That is the image of Christ's dying as a sacrifice. The New Testament is a Jewish collection of books, and sacrifice in this context must refer to the temple sacrifices offered on the altar in Jerusalem. I think we can see that all the images and theories I have listed are inextricably bound up with the key image of sacrifice. The slaves or captives who become sons and free are images above all of the children of Israel, once slaves in Egypt, whom God brought into the promised land. How did he free them? By getting them to sacrifice the passover lamb. The sinners who are justified in the great assize are justified by the blood of the Son of God (Rom 3.21-26). The love of the Son who gives his life for sinners is the love of one who willingly offers himself as a sacrifice to the Father. We distort the various metaphors we find in the New Testament if we try to interpret them without reference to the sacrificial Law of Moses.

The great scholar of Judaism, Paul Fiebig, in his striking pamphlet of 1906, *Jesu Blut, ein Geheimnis?* (Jesus' Blood, a Riddle [to which there is no answer?]), drew our attention to this simple fact about all the references in the New Testament to Jesus' blood: the blood is the blood of a sacrificial victim, a victim offering himself as a sacrifice, as sacrifice was understood in Judaism.

Fiebig went on, however, to argue that, by the time of Jesus, Jews had lost any clear understanding of how sacrifice worked. Sacrifice did work, as familiar ritual; and, because it worked, Jesus' death could work too. But neither Jesus nor those who preached Jesus made anything of how the sacrificial death operated. They did not want to, and they did not need to, because the symbolism still worked without explanation. Just as Jews concentrated on defining and refining the ritual without ever discussing the reason for the ritual, so Christian preachers could point to the actual sacrificial death of Christ without saying why the sacrificial death was necessary, and why it performed the atonement it obviously did perform.

From this conclusion Fiebig drew the inference that twentieth-century Christians did not need to bother their heads with explanations of how sacrifice worked in the first century; it did not work now, and, in any case, theories about how it worked *there* were wholly lacking and did not need to be supplied. Of course there were theories behind both Jewish and pagan sacrificial cults, but these theories belong to a childish stage of religion, when sin was regarded as a physical entity which could be loaded on to a victim, and when blood was life. We have outgrown this stage and can transmute anything spiritually valuable from the sacrificial cult into the language of an inner religion.

I agree with Fiebig that the one key image for the death of Christ in the New Testament was the image of his sacrificial offering of himself to the Father. I agree with Fiebig that Jesus and his contemporaries took it for granted that divinely-willed sacrifice worked. I disagree with Fiebig when he argues that no one clear theory of how the self-sacrifice of Christ worked was present in the minds of Jews who pondered the question.

Notice one tell-tale connection they made which argues they had a specific theory, a dogma. Almost casually, one writer, the author of First John, asserts that the death of Christ was a propitiation "not only for our sins but also for [the sins] of the whole world" (1 John 2.2; cf. John 3.16). Paul says, almost casually, God was reconciling *the world* to himself in Christ (2 Cor 5.19). The massive assumption that Christ died for all was the engine of a world mission, and still is. I think only a dogma, only a theory can explain the assumption that the death of Christ had to be proclaimed to all nations and to all subsequent generations.

Why is the New Testament doctrine of the death of Christ elusive? Not because there was a rich variety and confusion of many perhaps incompatible doctrines; there was only one doctrine, a doctrine about Christ's offering of himself as a sacrifice. Not because no one had bothered to be clear about the theory of it. No. The answer is, I believe, that everyone simply assumed a common agreed theory; and the Christians then argued that what the theory required had occurred, when Jesus allowed himself to be put to death by crucifixion. We have no clear exposition of this theory not because it was obscure, or recondite, or buried under tradition. We have no clear exposition of the theory because it was so obvious and well-known and agreed that no one needed to stop to expound it.

It seems almost incredible, though, that something so massive could be lost. You do not, in Edinburgh, mislay the Mound and the Castle, that everyone can see for miles around. Well, no. I do not think a massive doctrine of the atonement has been mislaid at all. It is just that people who think about doctrine and write about it have made themselves incapable of rightly reading the only sort of evidence that is available. We have read the evidence as though it was a complete legal code, or a constitution, in which all the details were given in full; or, when that failed, we have read the evidence as though it was the work of poets and imaginative thinkers like us who delight to bare their souls in literature. But none of the evidence is like that. It is all either folk-tale literature, or sayings of seers or sages, or digests of sermons and speeches, or rubrics for services of worship, or prayers, or scraps of liturgy, or official letters, or collections of proverbs, or targums, or psalms or chronicles. What everyone knows is not likely to be found explained, although traces of its presence will pop up everywhere.

If I am right, the only way we can see the obvious again is to have it blocked in for us. Then, if what is blocked in is true, we shall find indirect confirmation of its truth in all sorts of surprising places, as well as in the obvious places.

I suspect that a great number of Jews at the time of Christ held two related beliefs about the death of human beings as sacrifice, and that almost all Jews would know that these beliefs were held, even if they themselves did not subscribe to them.

The first belief was that righteous martyrs and would-be martyrs were effective in atoning for the sins of those they prayed for. Moses said to the people, "Ye have sinned a great sin: and now I will go up unto the Lord; peradventure I shall make an atonement for your sin." The atonement consisted in praying to be blotted out from the book of life (Ex 32.3-35). In this case, the prayer was not heard. Similarly David offered himself for the people's sin, as did Paul in Romans 9.1-5, as did Flavius Josephus (*War* 5.419), as did the righteous sectaries at Qumran (1QS 8.4-10; cf. 5.6; 1QSa 1.3), as did the Teacher of Righteousness (4Q541), as did the rabbis.[1] The willing sacrifice of Isaac for their sins was held up in prayer by the passover worshippers in Jerusalem on the second night of the passover; for was not the Temple built on Mount Moriah? In a Targum of Genesis 22, Abraham prayed,

> Now I pray for mercy before You, O Lord God, that when the children of Isaac come to a time of distress, You may remember on their behalf the binding of Isaac their father, and loose and forgive them their sins and deliver them from all distress, so that the generations which follow him may say: In the mountain of the Temple of the Lord, Abraham offered Isaac his

---

[1] For the rabbis, see Solomon Schechter (1909), pp. 310-311.

son, and in this mountain—of the Temple—the glory of the Shekhinah of the Lord was revealed to him.[2]

When the Maccabean martyrs died they died praying, like Eleazar,

> Be merciful to your people and let our punishment be a satisfaction on their behalf. Make my blood their purification, and take my soul to ransom their souls (4 Macc 6.28; cf. 17.21, 22).

The theology behind this belief was that the people who had failed to keep God's law were rightly suffering at the hand of God. The prophets had long taught the people not to blame circumstances or the enemy for their suffering but to see the suffering as the just consequence of their own sin. Psalm 106 is a litany of deserved punishment and draws special attention to the intercession of the righteous Moses and Phinehas for the people.

The martyr willingly took on himself the sufferings of his people and prayed for them as he died. He prayed his death might be a sacrifice for their sin. If his prayer were answered, God would give the people a respite from deserved suffering and the people would use the time in order to repent. They would take the martyr's death as their sacrifice to the Father for their sins, and would pray that the Father would remember Isaac or the other willing martyrs in their favour. "Do this in remembrance of me": Do this that sinners may pray the Father to remember my death for them.

The second belief many Jews at the time of Christ held, and perhaps all Jews knew was held, was a belief about the Messiah. According to that view, the eternal Son of God, the Lamb of God, was slain from the foundation of the world on a heavenly altar whenever the innocent were persecuted or suffering.

The evidence for this belief is sparse and scattered and difficult to interpret, but it is there. It is simply alluded to at the end of the sentence in Rev 13.8: "And all that dwell upon earth shall worship [the beast], whose names are not written in the book of life of the Lamb slain from the foundation of the world." (There are modern attempts to remove the words "from the foundation of the world" from the Lamb slain, but these attempts are not successful. The perfect tense of the participle, ἐσφαγμένου, does not refer to one slaying but to repeated slayings, as the perfect participle ἐκκεχυμένον in Luke 11.50 refers to the righteous blood continually poured out from Abel to Zachariah the son of Barachiah, Matt 23.35-36; Luke 11.50-51.) In

---

[2] Translated Vermes (1961), p. 195. Cf. Le Déaut (1963).

the midst of the throne stood the Lamb as it had been slain—ἐσφαγμένον, another perfect (Rev 5.6; cf. 5.12; 7.14 and τὸν ἀριθμὸν τῶν ἐσφαγισμένων, 7.4).

The saying of Jesus already referred to, that all the righteous blood shed on earth would come on his generation, from the blood of Abel to the blood of Zachariah (Matt 23.35-36; cf. Luke 11.50-51) is ascribed to The Wisdom of God in Luke and looks very like an old tradition that has been transferred to Jesus. It implies that the death of the righteous has been stored up and will now be required. But where stored up, if not in the sufferings of the Messiah from the foundation of the world?

The Messiah was always there in history because the Image of God was always there. The Stone had been laid to represent the continual presence of God with humanity and particularly with his people Israel. The Stone followed the wilderness generation, and eventually found its place in the Temple.

The Woes of the Messiah are the birth pangs or the sufferings of the people that will precede the coming of the Messiah (Isa 26.17; 66.8; Jer 22.23; Hos 13.13; Micah 4.9-10; 1QH 3.7-12). But, despite Billerbeck,[3] they are also the woes borne by the Messiah. Anyone who was busied with the Torah and the works of love would escape the woes of the Messiah, meaning would escape inflicting further woes on the Messiah that would in turn bring deliverance from suffering the woes of the Messiah when he came.

In the Psalms, David and David's greater son bear themselves the reproaches; the reproaches of those that reproached God are fallen on him (Psalm 69.7-9, 19; 89.50-51).

In *1 Enoch* 47 the blood of the Righteous One is brought to the Ancient of Days with the prayers of the righteous. As the prayers of the righteous for deliverance from their sufferings have continually ascended to God from the altar, so the blood of the Righteous One may well have been thought of as continually offered (*1 Enoch* 47.1-4; Rev 8.3-4; 5.8).[4]

The prophecy, "They will see me whom they have pierced" may well have been taken as a general prophecy that all the dead who were raised would see the one who was pierced at the time by their sins committed before their death (Zech 12.10).

---

[3] Billerbeck (1922), Vol. I, p. 950.
[4] Barker (1996), pp. 17-18; Black (1985), p. 209.

Matt 25 records the parable of the Sheep and the Goats. This parable is so unlike the other parables of Jesus that Jülicher did not include it in his great book on the parables.[5] It stems from old Jewish tradition, and turns on the fact that the sufferings of the least of the Son of Man's brethren are sufferings borne by the Son of Man as well as that the blessings experienced by the least of the brethren are also rejoiced in by the Son of Man. The persecution of the righteous on earth is matched by the suffering of the Son of Man in heaven.

Paul in his vision on the Damascus Road is asked why he is persecuting the Son of Man whom he heard Stephen say he saw as he died a martyr's death. The heavenly figure says, "Why are you persecuting me?" Paul is of course persecuting Jews who believed that Jesus was the Messiah; Paul must accept the logic of the question from heaven that the sufferings of the righteous amount to sufferings also inflicted on the Messiah. Once Paul has accepted that the heavenly figure is the Messiah, all he needs to know now is the identity of the Son of Man. So he asks, "Who are you, Lord?" (Acts 9.3-5; 22.6-8; 26.14-15).

The writer to the Hebrews taught that those who spurn the Son of God when they have tasted his mercy crucify him again for themselves and put him to open shame (Heb 6.6). Moses counted τὸν ὀνειδισμὸν τοῦ Χριστοῦ greater than the riches of Egypt. The reproach of Christ is more likely the reproach born by Christ in the sufferings of his enslaved people as they made the perilous journey to freedom than the reproach born for the sake of Christ (Heb 11.26). The rock that followed them was Christ (1 Cor 10.4). Let us not test Christ as some of them tested him and were destroyed by the serpents (1 Cor 10.9 as read by p^{46} D F G Ψ1739 1881 and the majority of mss.).

Finally, *Pesikta Rabbati* 31 (146b) should be cited. "One cannot say with how many sufferings the Messiah will be afflicted in every single generation for the sins of that generation. God says in that hour (Isa 49): I make him new, and no longer will he be afflicted by suffering." This is a late collection, but it seems unlikely that the tradition itself is recent because it would chime in with the Christian teaching about Jesus (cf. Melito of Sardis),[6] and would not for that reason commend itself to later generations of scholars of the Torah.

Heb 9.26 seems to contradict the view that the Messiah suffered from the foundation of the world. This is, I suspect, a misreading of

---

[5] Jülicher (1899), Vol. I, pp. viii-ix. This 2nd ed. of Vol. I was published after Vol. II, and this is Jülicher's answer to his critics on the omission.
[6] Lieu (1996), pp. 209-240.

Hebrews, stemming from the assumption that the discourses in Hebrews are the work of an author mounting an argument. They seem rather to be collections of pithy aphorisms, joined together because of general agreement of subject and particular connection by catchwords.

I think we should translate Heb 9.25-26 as follows.

> 9.25. Was it not [fitting] that he should offer himself often, as the high priest enters the holy of holies every year with the blood of another?
> New saying:
> 9.26. Since it was necessary that he should suffer many times from the foundation of the world, [the time is at last fulfilled]. And now at last [ἄπαξ] at the conclusion of the ages he has appeared [on earth] to put away sin [openly] by his sacrifice.

The catchwords that brought the two separate sayings together were *many times* [πολλάκις] in both verses, and *offer* [προσφέρῃ] in verse 25 matching *sacrifice* [διὰ τῆς θυσίας] in verse 26.

If this belief that the Messiah has always suffered and always will suffer till Judgment Day holds, then the incarnation and the crucifixion of the Son of God is the making visible once for all of the sacrifice of the Son of God in heaven. All sins before and since the incarnation are sins which lead to a heavenly sacrifice, a sacrifice that shows how much God loves both the righteous, who suffer, and the sinners who cause them to suffer. The sacrifice is to give the sinners time to repent, and to provide the sinners with an offering they can now make to the Father for their sins. So their sins are atoned, and they have peace with God.

This doctrine escapes the charges of arbitrariness often levelled against Anselm, and charges of God's immorality. This doctrine answers both the needs of sinners who realize they have done wrong and repent, and the needs of their victims, who wonder why the sinner sometimes escapes punishment.

I suspect that this massive double belief in the efficacy of martyrdom as sacrifice, and in the continuous suffering of the Messiah from the foundation of the world lies behind the whole New Testament. Everyone knew of it, and the New Testament believers proclaimed that Jesus was that Son of God who had died for the sins of the whole world. The Son of God was slain from the foundation of the world, and "Jesus Christ will be in agony until the end of the world" (Pascal).[7]

---

[7] Lafuma ed. 919 (1962), p. 378; Everyman translation, p. 148.

8

The Point of Christology

When I first called this book *The Point of It All* I had forgotten that Schubert M. Ogden's striking 1980 Sarum Lectures were published under the title *The Point of Christology*. In his Preface he stated that he had two kinds of persons in mind as he tried to fulfil the terms of the Sarum Lectureship: "those who regard themselves as non-Christians" because they have never been able to come to terms with the claims that Christians have historically made concerning Jesus himself; and "those who would like to think of themselves as Christians and who either accept or at least are powerfully attracted by the offer of faith that is re-presented to them through Jesus, only to continually doubt whether they can really call themselves Christians after all." To both listeners, he wanted to offer a "radical faith that is decisively re-presented to them through Jesus."[1]

Since I have exactly the same audience in mind, and since I regard Ogden as not only the most perceptive critic of Bultmann I know of, but also as an acute theologian in his own right, I offer a critical view of his teaching about Christ and argue that he is the heir of a tradition of thinking about Christ that is nearly two centuries old.

Schubert Ogden began by insisting that we should ask the question about the *truth* of christology, as well as the question about its *meaning*. He is surely right; but how do we know whether or not a proposed christology is true? Ogden says that an adequate christology must be credible, meaning "credible to human existence as judged by common experience and reason."[2] That, too, is surely right; christology must not contradict historical and scientific evidence, and not be illogical in any of its moves.

However, when we read further, we find that he turns out to mean more than just that. He has definite ideas of what scientific evi-

[1] Ogden (1982), p. x.
[2] Ogden (1982), p. 4.

dence and historical evidence teaches. He seems to think that Bultmann held a modern scientific world-picture;[3] and he seems to think that modern historical consciousness entails "an explicit awareness that human beings create themselves and one another, by creating their own social and cultural orders."[4] I should have thought that neither of these is obvious. On the second, anyone who thinks he can take "an emancipatory resolve to transform the conditions of human existence" has obviously not considered what he is up against: not only chance; not only the strategic uncertainty of not knowing how his opponents or partners will react; but also the radical uncertainty which consists of ignorance of possible qualitative changes.[5] Ogden seems not to have thought of new inventions, or of any other sort of surprise as being devastatingly important in history, and radically uncertain. Although his particular list of what is credible strikes me as incredible, it remains true that his tests are right; an adequate christology should be credible; and "credible" means, in accordance with historical and scientific evidence, interpreted logically.

Why, then, does Ogden add yet another criterion of truth to these two? What more is there to say about any system of thought than that it is credible to those who are prepared to judge impartially of its truth?

Ogden's other criterion is the criterion of appropriateness. He means that a critical reflective christology must interpret the meaning of spontaneous direct confessions about Jesus in a way that is *appropriate* to the norm of what the earliest apostles believed.[6]

His problem is to maintain a connection between his present-day christology and the christology of the past. He finds Chalcedonian christology too problematic to be worth defending, and he rejects the *revisionary* christologies that still ask, Who is Jesus?; which think Christ is the historical Jesus; and which think Jesus had himself to actualize the possibility of self-understanding.[7]

He plumps instead for what the apostles believed about Jesus as his norm, and connects his own modern christology with that norm by the criterion of appropriateness.

---

[3] Ogden (1982), p. 6.
[4] Ogdon (1982), pp. 89-90.
[5] Burns (1968), chapter 2: "Real Uncertainty and Surprise: The Consequences in Politics."
[6] Ogden (1982), p. 4, and the longer discussion on pp. 96-105 and the whole of chapter 6.
[7] Ogden (1982), pp. 15-19.

Notice two presuppositions. He presupposes, he takes for granted, that the christological thoughts of the apostles were different from the thoughts of Jesus, and different from the thoughts of later parts of the canon, and different from the thoughts of the early church councils, and different from the thoughts of the advocates of revisionary christologies.

His second presupposition is more complicated. He also presupposes that his own thoughts are different from the thoughts of the apostles: the apostles used "terms and categories" which are mythological—talk of the cross (in the case of Paul) and terms and categories from apocalyptic eschatology (in the case of the earliest witness to Jesus). He also argues that we have to demythologize them. But *his* thoughts are "appropriate", because they are appropriate to the "basic motif" "implicit" in these early normative christologies.[8]

What, then, is the "basic motif" to which Ogden's own christology is appropriate? The "basic motif" is "Jesus who means love and, therefore, also means freedom, because, being the gift and demand of God's [boundless] love made fully explicit, he is the decisive representation of our own possibility to be truly free."[9] He believes he is distinguishing between "the constitutive christological assertion itself" (the sort of thing I have just cited) and "any particular christological formulation that makes or implies it."[10]

Now we see why he needs a second criterion of truth over and above the criterion of credibility. Credibility attaches only to thoughts (in Frege's usage of "thoughts"). All past thoughts are incredible, including the thoughts of the apostles. But christology, in order to go on calling itself christology, and in order to allow its holders to lay claim to the wealth and power of the church and the wealth and power the state still allows to the church, must maintain continuity with some norm or other in the past which can be plausibly be maintained to be normative christology. What better device than "appropriateness," since those who can get others to recognize that they act appropriately, may appropriate to themselves the honour and power associated with the body in which they do the right thing.

If a critic should ask Ogden whether it was credible that his christology was the same as the christology of the apostles, he would reply that his christology was appropriate. Credibility is the test of "human

---

[8] Ogden (1982), pp. 124-125.
[9] Ogden (1982), p. 125; for *boundless* love, see pp. 118ff., 139, 145 *et passim*.
[10] Ogden (1982), p. 22.

existence as judged by common experience and reason"; the looser test of appropriateness is the only test required to establish that his christology *is* the christology of the apostles. By "appropriate" he means that his christology shares the same "basic motif" of the christology of the apostles, once we discard the mythological particular formulations. I take this to mean the apostles would not have recognized Ogden's picture, although we can now see that this was what they were really getting at.

The very criterion of appropriateness, distinct from the criterion of credibility, is an attempt to establish another sort of continuity than truth, and another sort of value than truth, the value which one can preserve by speaking and acting appropriately.

"God is boundless love" may look like a thought which could be true or false, but it is not. It is "a symbolic metaphysical claim" which asserts that "God" is acted on by everything as well as acting on everything,[11] and obviously such a thought cannot be true or false, because the very decision one way or the other will change "God", since "God is acted on by everything."

Ogden is a typical theologian. He appeals to a "consensus" of "scholars" in order to establish this basic motif of apostolic belief.[12] He assumes that these scholars are all busy burrowing away under the specific beliefs of the apostles to something more basic, and he is surely right. What they find is always relational and undefined. Ogden appeals to scholars who think the apostles taught faith in God's boundless love, a boundless love of God for them demanding their boundless love for others. He describes this new existence as "the freedom we have in Christ"[13] and the constructive part of the book is devoted to working out the behaviour appropriate to this "freedom we have in Christ."

Had Ogden been working more closely with Paul rather than with the Gospel material he could just as easily found a scholarly consensus which would have offered him a similar "basic motif." E.P.Sanders argues that "the basic insight" in Paul's thought "was that the believer becomes one with Christ Jesus and that this effects a transfer of lordship, and the beginning of a transformation which will be completed with the coming of the Lord."[14] Becoming one with Christ Jesus is basic. C.F.D. Moule puts a similar point.

---

[11] Ogden (1982), p. 145.
[12] Ogden (1982), pp. 115-120.
[13] Ogden (1982), pp. 166, 167.
[14] Sanders (1977), p. 549; cf. his careful restatement (1983), pp. 4-15.

> Paul ... had religious experiences in which the Jesus of Nazareth who had recently been crucified ... was found to more than individual. He was found to be an "inclusive" personality. And this means, in effect, that Paul was led to conceive of Christ as any theist conceives of God: personal, indeed, but transcending the individual category. Christ is like the omnipresent deity "in whom we live and move and have our being"...[15]

Moule argues that this is not one christology among many, but that here we are at the roots of christology. All the New Testament conceptions of Jesus are "'true' to the Person, Jesus himself,"[16] but to "Jesus as more than individual, as transcendent and eternal and all comprehensive,"[17] to "Jesus ... as an inclusive, Israel-wide—indeed, Adam-wide—person: one who, as no merely human individual, included persons and communities within him, and upon whom Christians found converging all the patterns of relationship between God and man with which they were familiar from their Scriptures."[18]

I do not deny that Jesus was taken to teach that God loved sinners and wished sinners to love their neighbours; nor do I deny that Paul taught that Christ transferred sinners from this evil age and transformed their lives; nor do I deny that the apostles wished to be true to Jesus and to belong with him.

The point is that all three writers, and the great Albert Schweitzer whose ideas lie behind all three positions, are not arguing for these propositions as *some* propositions among the many that make up the apostolic christology; they distinguish their themes as "the basic motif," as "the basic insight," as lying at the "roots" of all else.

We should be grateful to Ogden for bringing out the characteristic feature of this "basic motif": this sort of basic motif is specifically designed to be a norm to which our contemporary christology can be "appropriate." For if the norm is completely all-embracing and entirely lacking in specific content, we *must* be able to relate ourselves to that norm in an appropriate way. We are told to demythologize all specific "terms and categories" and to commit ourselves to God as boundless love; or we are to live the "Christian life ... in an area which is Christ," in Christ as an "inclusive personality."[19] All we have to do is to surrender ourselves to union with something that is defined as without bounds or definite distinctions; "the ultimate reality

---

[15] Moule (1977), p. 95.
[16] Moule (1977), p. 135.
[17] Moule (1977), p. 142.
[18] Moule (1977), p. 136.
[19] Moule (1977), p. 95.

called 'God' is the strictly universal individual whose boundless love for all things is their sole primal source as well as their only final end."[20]

This demand was a nineteenth-century commonplace. Schleiermacher canonized it for the church: "the appearance of Christ and the institution of this new corporate life ... [is] the completion ... of the creation of human nature."[21] But it crops up everywhere, as much in Comte's "religion of humanity" as in the Communist Manifesto. Comte divided human history into three periods, each succeeding the other: the theological, when everything is explained as due to supernatural beings (gods, spirits and so on); the metaphysical, when everything was explained as due to abstract forces inherent in all things (substances, attributes, monads and so on); and the positive, which began about 1788, when everything is explained as subjected to invariable natural laws and all we can do is to analyse phenomena and connect them by natural laws of succession and resemblance. The Cambridge New Testament scholar Brooke Foss Westcott (1825-1901) used Comte's thought to turn away from all metaphysical dogmas and to adopt a Christianity centred on Christ as the all-inclusive centre of the new humanity.

> Christ, as He is revealed to us, in His Life, His Death, His Resurrection, is the One Mediator by Whom every blessing comes; the one all-containing Presence by Whom men are bound together. In His Person every difference of race, of station, of nature, is done away. "In Christ", to use the favourite phrase of the Apostle, our whole life and being and work are centred.[22]

The Ariadne thread is the worship of the creative process of history by which the new humanity is created, and the commitment to that process and to nothing else. Its one principle is that there are no principles, only commitment to the way mankind is making itself. The only question is, What is appropriate to that?

This view is incoherent, because no amount of rhetoric can show us that opportunism is a principle, or that any system that eschews truths which do not change can be true.

But incoherent systems have existed in various ages in the past, and we can rightly ask whether the positions advocated by Ogden and the others actually did exist in the minds of Jesus and the apostles. Was

---

[20] Ogden (1982), p. 131.
[21] Schleiermacher (1830), §89; English trans. p. 366.
[22] Westcott (1866), 3rd ed. (1874), p. 126.

their christology of this all-inclusive and indeterminate kind; were the "terms and categories" they used in fact only superficial, and easily removed; was the "basic motif" what they say it was, purely relational?

Take Jesus first. Ogden conceded that Jesus used the mythology of Jewish apocalypticism "whose terms and categories were well known and well used by many persons in Jesus' day whose answer to the existential question was significantly different from his own." But in Jesus' case that use was purely formal. "All that it can say is what it served to say to his hearers—namely, that the ultimate reality by which their existence was finally determined was none other than the God whose gift and demand were already confronting them through Jesus himself with the definitive decision for or against their own authentic existence." God was the God of boundless love who demanded faith in this boundless love. The reign of God is the reign of boundless love. Those who receive the love must respond with a like love, which is also boundless. The will of God is sharply set over against traditional requirements of the law.[23] The aim is that everyone should become "active subjects of their own self-creation, instead of merely passive objects of the self-creations of others."[24]

As we have seen in the chapter on Jesus' parables, Jesus believed that human beings were required to live by God's laws revealed through Moses and the prophets, and that everyone would some day have to answer to God for the life they had lived. He did teach that God loves every human being and that every human being should love like God, but he also taught that everyone had to use the time given them by God's goodness in order to prepare themselves to meet God's judgment. There is a boundary, a limit, an end to forbearance, and the teaching of Jesus and his death were designed to enable everyone to meet that end and live. Jesus acted as messiah, and that implied that God's love is conditional and his forbearance limited. Human beings were created by God; their end is not to become "active subjects of their own self-creation" but joyful worshippers of the God who made them and who loves them and wants them to be free, but who will require an account of their stewardship at the end.

If Jesus' teaching is not reducible to Ogden's theology, nor is the teaching of the Pauline corpus of writings reducible to his terms.

---

[23] Ogden (1982), pp. 117-119.
[24] Ogden (1982), p. 123.

Nowhere in the New Testament, least of all in the Pauline writings, is Christ thought of an an inclusive person in whom all Christians live.

The most influential advocate of this view was Adolf Deissmann. His book *Die neutestamentliche Formel "in Christo Jesu"* was his inaugural dissertation as a Privatdocent (lecturer) in the University of Marburg in 1892. Like the other scholars we have been considering, from Schleiermacher to Ogden, he wanted to argue that the formula "in Christ" was not just one of the many thoughts of Paul.

> We have here one of the favourite ideas—or, better still, *the* favourite idea in the religious language of the Apostle. Paul formed this term in order to express something peculiar to him, which interested only him; ... by using a manner of speech that was already to hand [the occasional use of the preposition ἐν (*in*) with personal singular noun or pronoun], he created an entirely new *terminus technicus*.[25]

Deissmann's reason for arguing that the phrase *in Christ* has one constant technical meaning is simple. He argues, positively, that ordinary Greek uses *in* with a singular personal noun or pronoun only in a psychological or forensic sense, both of which senses are basically local. For example, Socrates says to Phaedo, "When you say that Simmias is taller than Socrates, and smaller than Phaedo, aren't you saying that both qualities are *in Simmias*, both tallness and smallness?" (Phaedo 102B) Negatively Deissmann argues that Greek-speaking Jews never used *in* with a singular personal noun or pronoun in any other sense, except when mechanically translating from a Hebrew or Aramaic original. Paul, in particular, although drawing on the LXX for vocabulary, was almost completely uninfluenced by the syntax of the LXX translators. As Deissmann said, "Granted that the gospel was foolishness to the Greeks, yet the most successful herald of the gospel was not so foolish as to offer it to the Greeks in un-Greek clothing."[26]

From these two premises, one positive and the other negative, it follows that the phrase is not standard Greek, and must be understood according to standard Greek usage in a local sense. Ordinary Greek could not have said that men were *in* a god, and yet ordinary Greek usage, which Paul was following, would have to understand the phrase *in Christ* in precisely this local sense; *in* with a singular personal noun or pronoun must be local.

On the basis of his elegant and seemingly rigorous argument about language, Deissmann asserted that one had to assume from the start

---

[25] Deissmann (1892), p. 70.
[26] Deissmann (1892), p. 67.

that *in Christ* was a formula and that it had a local meaning. He assumed that Paul thought of the nature of the exalted Christ as spiritual, and that when he said Christians were *in Christ* he meant that they lived in Christ as in an "element", as an animal lives "in" the air, as fish "in" water, or as the roots of plants "in" the soil.[27]

Table of possible meanings of ἐν with a singular name or title or with a singular personal pronoun

I ἐν refers to a person as a place
1. in, among: Deut 15.4 LXX (singular=collective)
2. to: 1 Kgs 1.26; 3 Kgs 22.28 Ps 84.9; Hos 1.2; *PsSol* 5.15; Matt 17.12 & par.; 1 Cor 14.11; Gal 1.16a.
3. with: Ps 13.5; Isa 45.14; *PsSol* 14.2; *TJos* 10.3; *TBen* 10.11; 1 Cor 15.18; 2 Cor 14.4b; 1 Thess 4.17(B); Ign *Eph* 20.2.
4. towards: 1 Clem 49.1 cf. 47.6; 48.4.
5. upon: Josh 6.26; 3 Kgs 16.34; Ps 55.13 (56.12).
6. in relation to, before: 1 Sam 23.16; *TNaph* 8.10; Philo *det.pot.* 48.
7. of, belonging to, available to: John 11.10; 1 Cor 7.39; 1 Thess 1.1; Eph 6.21; Herm *mand.* 4.1.4; Ign *Trall* 8.2; Sophocles *Oedipus Rex Tyrannus* 314.
8. against: Dan 11.30; John 14.30

II ἐν refers to a person as the origin or the means or the object of an action
1. with verbs of boasting (in), hoping (in), swearing (by) PsSol 17.1; 3 Kgs 1.30
2. with verbs of trusting, believing (in)
3. by means of, through: 2 Cor 2.12; Ezek 38.16; in the power of: Ps 17.30; 43.6; 59.14; with the help of: John 3.21
4. because of, on account of: Matt 13.57; *TLevi* 18.5,9; Gal 1.24
5. to ask from (origin): Judges 20.28 (B); 1 Kgs 10.22; *TJud* 24.6
6. by (agent): Isa 45.26; Gal 3.14
7. in the case of, with respect to, for, about: Matt 10.32; 17.12
8. on behalf of, for, in the service of: *TLevi* 7.1; Ps 68.18 (67.19); Eus *HE* 5.24.7; Rom 16.6b.

---

[27] Deissmann (1892), pp. 81-82, 84-85.

Deissmann's argument scarcely holds. If we can find a couple of instances in Paul where Paul does not use *in* with a singular personal pronoun to represent a local sense, which is, according to Deissmann, required by standard Greek usage, then we have proved that Paul did not always follow standard Greek usage. If he did not bind himself to follow standard Greek usage, it is highly unlikely that he thought he was doing anything peculiar and strange and new by writing something impossible to a standard Greek writer, namely *in Christ*. He is unlikely to mean *in Christ* to be a formula; he is unlikely to think of himself as creating a new technical phrase.

In the Table at I,2 and II,4 there are two verses from Paul where he writes ἐν ἐμοί meaning *to me* (*God was pleased to reveal his Son to me*; Gal 1.16a) and ἐν ἐμοί meaning *because of me* (*the churches glorified God because of me*; Gal 1.24). Deissmann's theory cannot, therefore, stand as a whole because here are two examples of the preposition *in* with a singular personal pronoun which does not treat that pronoun as representing a space in which anyone resides.

However, it may still be true that Paul sometimes used the phrase *in Christ* in the sense that Deissmann thought always went with the usage; perhaps sometimes Paul treated Christ as a spiritual element in which people lived. The Table is designed to show that the only cases in the Greek of the Old and New Testaments and in related Greek which come close to what Deissmann took to be the general rule are cases in which ἐν with a singular name or title or pronoun referring to a person clearly refers to a collective (I,1). Deut 15.4 says ὅτι οὐκ ἔσται ἐν σοὶ ἐνδεής, *for there shall not be a poor person in you, among you*, where the singular ἐν σοί refers to the people of Israel. Otherwise, ἐν always means something different. Perhaps the most surprising set is I,3, where ἐν seems to mean *with*. A good case is *TBen* 10.11: "As for you, if you go in holiness before the face of the Lord you will again dwell in hope *with me* (ἐν ἐμοί) and all Israel will be gathered to the Lord." Another important set is I,7 where ἐν seems to mean *of*. A good example is Ignatius *to the Trallians* 8.2: "Do not give opportunities to the Gentiles [by your harbouring grudges against one another] lest the congregation of God be blasphemed because of a few foolish people (τὸ ἐν θεῷ πλῆθος)."

Finally, consider II,3. The group from the Psalms where ἐν seems to mean *in the power of* or *by* was drawn to my attention by Athanasius, *Four Discourses against the Arians* 3.21, so the problem and the solution are not new: "By God we shall do a miracle"; "by God I shall leap over a wall"; "by you shall we tread down our enemies" (LXX Ps 59.14; 17.30; 43.6).

Further confirmation that we are on the right lines is provided by the scribes who changed ἐν for some other preposition (or some other preposition for ἐν); this is near-contemporary evidence of native Greek speakers who understood ἐν in the senses we have suggested. So under I,2 some manuscripts have a simple dative instead of ἐν with the dative at 1 Cor 14.11.[28]

Despite all these arguments, there remain about ten passages in the New Testament where most commentators agree that ἐν Χριστῷ or the like means *in Christ*, Christ being spoken of as the *locus* in which believers dwell. These passages are: Rom 8.1; 16.7; 1 Cor 15.22; 2 Cor 5.17; Gal 1.22; Phil 1.1; 3.8-9; 1 Thess 1.1; 2.14; 2 Thess 1.1.

I shall take the two most often-quoted passages to see whether or not they must really be read as meaning *in Christ*. They are 1 Cor 15.22 and 2 Cor 5.17.

> For as through a man death,
> so through a man the resurrection of the dead;
> for as *in Adam* all die,
> so also *in Christ* all shall be made alive.
> (1 Cor 15.21-22)

It is natural to take verse 22 as repeating the thought of verse 21, but now adding the names; verse 21 says δι' ἀνθρώπου twice, and verse 22 would seem to continue on the same lines, using ἐν with the dative to mean the same as διά with the genitive (II,3 in the Table): as through Adam all die, so through Christ shall all be made alive.

Two further arguments confirm this translation. First, the references to *all* in both halves of verse 22 are very much easier to understand if ἐν means *through* than if ἐν means *in*. If ἐν means *in*, we must take the first occurrence of *all* as referring to all people without exception, and the second *all* as referring only to those who are truly *in Christ* by faith and baptism. But if we read ἐν as *through*, we can understand the word *all* in both cases to refer to all people: through

---

[28] I,3: σύν 1 Thess 4.17; 2 Cor 13.4; I,5: ἐπί Matt 13.57; Luke 2.40; *TJos* 10.3; I,7: εἰς Χριστόν 2 Cor 11.3; simple genitive and no preposition Rev 1.9; I,9: ἐπί, εἰς Matt 17.12; II,1: ἐπί Ps 55.4; simple dative and no preposition Matt 21.32; II,3: διά 1 Thess 4.2; John 9.3 = Pseudo-Clem. *Hom.* 19.22.6; II,5: ἐκ *TJud* 24.6; II,7: simple dative and no preposition *TNaph* 8.10; εἰς Matt 26.10=Mark 14.6. In some cases, parallel versions of a saying offer variants for ἐν.

Adam's sin they all die; and through Christ's power they shall all rise, some to eternal life and some to condemnation.

Second, the idea that all people are somehow incorporated into Adam, and that Adam is an inclusive personality has not yet been found in Jewish literature, although there are plenty of references to the universal effect of his sin. "O Adam, what have you done? For though it was you who sinned, the fall was not yours alone, but ours also who are your descendants" (*4 Ezra* 7.118 [2 Esdras 7.48]). Why do we have to make Paul invent a new concept about Adam in order to provide a foil for another allegedly new concept about Christ as an inclusive sphere of existence? Why don't we relax, and let the words bear a perfectly natural sense which any Jew would have understood, whether or not he would have agreed? Why are we so intent on saying that Paul had a new religion which was not Judaism? Surely *he* thought he had the only true Judaism.

We are completely accustomed to hearing 2 Cor 5.17 punctuated like this:

> Therefore if anyone is in Christ
> he is [*or* there is] a new creation;
> old things are passed away;
> behold, [they are become] new.

However, the only reason for this punctuation is the dogmatic resolve to translate ἐν Χριστῷ as *in Christ* and to relate *in Christ* tightly to *if anyone is*, εἴ τις. In any other sentence that began with *if*, we should try to make a proper protasis of all possible words down to the main verb of the apodosis: if such-and-such, then old things have passed away. If we take ἐν according to the category II,3, we get perfect sense:

> So if any one is a new creation through Christ,
> then the old things have passed away;
> behold, [the old things] are become new.

This was how Marcion, Tertullian (*Adv. Marc.* 5.12.6), and the Latin Vulgate took the sentence, and the translation is defended by Bachmann and Héring.[29]

In support of this reading, notice that in the Bible creation entails a creator. The translation I have offered mentions a creator, Christ, while the familiar translation has no creator, only a sphere of existence to walk round in.

---

[29] Bachmann (1909); Héring (1958), English trans. p. 43.

I have argued that Ogden by adding appropriateness as a test of the truth of christology to the proper criterion of credibility has given the game away. He want to discover, and does discover, in the New Testament a christology which only requires the response of now saying and doing the appropriate thing, and does not raise the awkward questions about truth; for if the primitive christology were true, it would still be true, and we could do nothing about it. We should have either to accept its truth or give up the positions of power and authority and influence our allegiance to Christianity still bestows on us.

I then argued that this relational "basic motif" Ogden finds in the apostolic witness belongs to a set of similar basic motifs, all of which imply that there is a force at work in the history of humanity with which the prudent should throw in their lot: we should all be devotees of the religion of humanity and discover the appropriate modern response to the ever-moving force of humanity advancing towards self-consciousness.

Finally, I asked whether one way of putting this motif in christology, the special translation of the term *in Christ*, really did hold true; whether Paul or anyone else really said that we should simply transfer our allegiance to Christ so that we were incorporated in him. I gave reasons for thinking that he never said this.

It turns out that this nineteenth-century view of the New Testament, still strongly preached in the twentieth century, is a construct which has no footing in the text. What is in the text is the simple statement that Christ died for sinners.

Bibliography

Ayers, M.R.
   1968   *The Refutation of Determinism.* London: Methuen.

Bachmann, Philipp
   1909   *Der zweite Brief des Paulus an die Korinther.* Kommentar zum Neuen Testament VIII. Leipzig: A. Deichert.

Barker, Margaret
   1996   "Atonement: The Rite of Healing." *Scottish Journal of Theology,* 49. Pp. 1-20.

Barrett, C.K.
   1994   *A Critical and Exegetical Commentary on The Acts of the Apostles.* Volume 1. Edinburgh: T. & T. Clark.

Barth, Karl
   1920   *Der Christ in der Gesellschaft: Eine Tambacher Rede.* Würzburg or München.
   1922   *Der Römerbrief.* New Revision. München: Chr. Kaiser. English translation: *The Epistle to the Romans,* translated from the sixth edition. London: Oxford University Press, 1933.
   1923   "Fünfzehn Antworten an Herrn Prof. von Harnack." *Christliche Welt,* 37. No. 5/6, 8 February, col. 8. Repr. *Theologische Fragen und Antworten. Gessammelte Vorträge.* 3.Band. Zollikon: Evangelischer Verlag, 1957. Pp. 7-31. English translation: H. Martin Rumscheidt. *Revelation and Theology. An Analysis of the Barth-Harnack Correspondence of 1923.* Cambridge: Cambridge University Press, 1972. Pp. 29-53 for Barth's text.
   1925   *Die Auferstehung der Toten: Eine akademische Vorlesung über 1. Kor. 15 (SS. 1923).* München. 2nd ed., 1926.
   1927   *Die christliche Dogmatik im Entwurf.* 1.Band: *Die Lehre vom Worte Gottes: Prolegomena zur christlichen Dogmatik.* München: Chr. Kaiser..
   1938   *Die kirchliche Dogmatik.* 1. Band. 2. Halbband. *Die Lehre vom Worte Gottes: Prolegomena zur kirchlichen Dogmatik.* Zollikon: Evangelische Buchhandlung. *Church Dogmatics.* Vol. 1. Second Half-Vol. *The Doctrine of the Word of God.* Ed. G.W. Bromiley, T.F. Torrance. Edinburgh: T&T Clark, 1956
   1940   *Die kirchliche Dogmatik.* 2. Band: *Die Lehre von Gott.* 1. Halbband. Zollikon-Zürich: Evangelischer Verlag. English translation: T.H.L. Parker, W.B. Johnston, Harold Knight, J.L.M. Haire. *Church Dogmatics*

II/1. *The Doctrine of God*. First Half-Volume. Edinburgh: T&T Clark, 1957.

1942 *Die kirchliche Dogmatik*. 2. Band: *Die Lehre von Gott*. 2.Halbband. Zollikon-Zürich: Evangelischer Verlag. English Translation: G.W. Bromiley, J.C. Campbell, Iain Wilson, J. Strathearn McNab, Harold Knight, R.A. Stewart. *Church Dogmatics* II/2. *The Doctrine of God*. Edinburgh: T&T Clark, 1957.

1947 *Die protestantische Theologie im 19. Jahrhundert: Ihre Vorgeschichte und ihre Geschichte*. Zürich: Evangelischer Verlag. English: *From Rousseau to Ritschl being the translation of eleven chapters of Die protestantische Theologie im 19. Jahrhundert*. The Library of Philosophy and Theology. London: SCM, 1959.

1948a *Die kirchliche Dogmatik*. 3. Band: *Die Lehre von der Schöpfung*; 2. Halbband. Zollikon, Zürich: Evangelischer Verlag. English Translation: Harold Knight, G.W. Bromiley, J.K.S. Reid, R.H. Fuller. *The Doctrine of Creation*. Edinburgh: T&T Clark, 1960.

1948b *Das christliche Verständnis der Offenbarung: Eine Vorlesung*. Theologische Existenz Heute. New series, No. 12. München. [A course of open lectures in Bonn, Summer Semester, 1947.] Translated as "The Christian Understanding of Revelation". *Against the Stream. Shorter Post-War Writings 1946-52*. Ed. Ronald Gregor Smith. London: SCM Press, 1954. Pp. 205-240.

1950 *Die kirchliche Dogmatik*. 3. Band. *Die Lehre von der Schöpfung*. 3. Teil. Zollikon-Zürich: Evangelischer Verlag. English Translation: G.W. Bromiley, R.J. Ehrlich. *Church Dogmatics* III,3. *The Doctrine of Creation*. Edinburgh: T&T Clark, 1961.

1955 *Die kirchliche Dogmatik*. 4. Band: *Die Lehre von der Versöhnung*. 2. Teil. Zollikon-Zürich: Evangelischer Verlag. English Translation: G.W. Bromiley. *The Doctrine of Reconciliation*. Edinburgh: T&T Clark, 1958.

1963 *Gebete*. München: Chr. Kaiser.

1971 *Karl Barth—Rudolf Bultmann Briefwechsel 1922-1966*. Ed. Jaspert. Gesamtausgabe. V, Bd. 1. Zürich: Theologischer Verlag. 2. revidierte und erweiterte Auflage. *Karl Barth—Rudolf Bultmann Briefwechsel 1911-1966*, 1994.

Bauckham, Richard

1998 "The Scrupulous Priest and the Good Samaritan: Jesus' Parabolic Interpretation of the Law of Moses." *New Testament Studies* 44. Pp. 475-489.

Beckett, Samuel

1958 *Endgame: A Play in one Act followed by ACT WITHOUT WORDS: A Mime for One Player*. Translated from the original French by the author. London: Faber and Faber, 1958. Paper covered edition, 1964.

Berger, Klaus
  1976 *Die Auferstehung des Propheten und die Erhöhung des Menschensohnes: Traditionsgeschichtliche Untersuchungen zur Deutung des Geschickes Jesu in frühchristlichen Texten*. Studien zur Umwelt des Neuen Testaments, 13. Göttingen: Vandenhoeck & Ruprecht.

Bernstein, Peter L.
  1996 *Against the Gods: The Remarkable Story of Risk*. New York: John Wiley & Sons, Inc.

Billerbeck, Paul and Strack, Hermann L.
  1922 *Kommentar zum Neuen Testament aus Talmud und Midrasch*. Erster Doppel-Band. *Das Evangelium nach Matthäus*. München: Beck. As one volume, 1926. Repr. 1982.

Black, Matthew
  1985 *The Book of Enoch or I Enoch. A New English Edition with commentary and textual notes*. In consultation with James C. VanderKam. Studia in Veteris Testamenti Pseudepigrapha, 7. Leiden: Brill.

Bloch, Ernst
  1923 *Geist der Utopie*. 2nd. ed. Berlin.

Borg, Marcus J.
  1987 *Jesus: A New Vision. Spirit, Culture, and the Life of Discipleship*. San Francisco: Harper & Row.
  1994 *Meeting Jesus Again for the First Time*. San Francisco: HarperCollins.

Bousset, Wilhelm
  1895 *Der Antichrist in der Überlieferung des Judentums, des neuen Testaments und der alten Kirche. Ein Beitrag zur Auslegung der Apocalypse*. Göttingen: Vandenhoeck & Ruprecht. English translation: *The Antichrist Legend: A Chapter in Christian and Jewish Folklore*. London: Hutchinson, 1896.
  1926 *Die Religion des Judentums im späthellenistischen Zeitalter*. 3rd ed. by Hugo Gressmann. Handbuch zum Neuen Testament, 21. Tübingen: J.C.B. Mohr (Paul Siebeck).

Burkitt, F.C.
  1903 "Text and Versions." *Encyclopaedia Biblica*. London: Adam and Charles Black. Published in four volumes, 1899-1903. One volume, 1903; corrected, 1914. Pp. 4977-5031.
  1929 "The Parable of the Ten Virgins." *The Journal of Theological Studies*, 30. Pp. 267-270

Burns, Arthur Lee
  1968 *Of Powers and Their Politics: A Critique of Theoretical Approaches*. Prentice-Hall Contemporary Political Theory Series. Englewood Cliffs, NJ: Prentice-Hall.

Campbell, C.A.
  1957 *On Selfhood and Godhood: The Gifford Lectures delivered at the University of St. Andrews during Sessions 1953-54 and 1954-55 revised and expanded*. Muirhead Library of Philosophy. London: Geo. Allen & Unwin.

Chadwick, Henry
: 1953 *Origen: Contra Celsum translated with an Introduction and Notes*. Cambridge: Cambridge University Press.

Charles, R.H.
: 1902 *The Book of Jubilees or Little Genesis*. London. Repr. Jerusalem, 1972.
: 1913 *The Apocrypha and Pseudepigrapha of the Old Testament in English with introductions and critical and explanatory notes to the several books*. Edited in conjunction with many scholars. Vol. II *Pseudepigrapha*. Oxford: Clarendon Press.

Charlesworth, James H.
: 1979 "The Concept of the Messiah in the Pseudepigrapha." *Aufstieg und Niedergang der römischen Welt*. II Principat. 19. Band. 1. Halbband: Religion (Judentum: Allgemeines; Palästinisches Judentum). Ed. Wolfgang Haase. Berlin: Walter de Gruyter. Pp. 188-218.
: 1992 *The Messiah: Developments in Earliest Judaism and Christianity*, Princeton Symposium. Minneapolis: Fortress.

Clarke, W.K. Lowther
: 1929 *New Testament Problems: Essays—Reviews—Interpretations*. London: Society for Promoting Christian Knowledge.

Collins, John J.
: 1995 *The Scepter and the Star. The Messiahs of the Dead Sea Scrolls and Other Ancient Literature*. The Anchor Bible Reference Library. New York: Doubleday.

Crossan, John Dominic
: 1991 *The Historical Jesus: The Life of a Jewish Mediterranean Peasant*. San Francisco: HarperCollins.
: 1993 *Jesus: A Revolutionary Biography*. San Francisco: HarperCollins.

Dalman, G.H.
: 1888 *Der leidende und der sterbende Messias der Synagoge im ersten nachchristlichen Jahrtausend*. Schriften des Institutum Judaicum in Berlin, 4. Berlin: H. Reuther.

Danby, Herbert
: 1933 *The Mishnah translated from the Hebrew with Introduction and brief explanatory notes*. Oxford: Clarendon Press.

Daube, David
: 1994 "Judas", *Rechtshistorisches Journal* 13. Pp. 307-330.

Deatrick, Eugene P.
: 1962 "Salt, Soil, Savior." *The Biblical Archaeologist* 25. Pp. 41-48.

Deissmann, G. Adolf
: 1892 *Die neutestamentliche Formel "in Christo Jesu"*. Marburg: N.G. Elwert.

de Jonge, M.
: 1986 "Two Messiahs in the Testaments of the Twelve Patriarchs?" *Tradition and Re-Interpretation in Jewish and Early Christian Literature: Essays in Honour of Jürgen C.H. Lebram*. Edited by J.W. van Henten, H.J. de Jonge, P.T van Rooden, J.W. Wesselius. Leiden: Brill. Pp. 150-162.

Dodd, C.H.
   1935 *The Parables of the Kingdom*. London: Nisbet. Revised ed., London: Fontana, 1961.
Downing, Gerald
   1987 *Jesus and the Threat of Freedom*. London: SCM.
   1988 *Christ and the Cynics*. Sheffield: Sheffield Academic Press.
   1992 *Cynics and Christian Origins*. Edinburgh: T. & T. Clark.
Dupont-Sommer, André
   1961 *The Essene Writings from Qumran*. Translated by G. Vermes from the 2nd ed. of *Les Ecrits esséniens découverts près de la mer Morte*, Paris.
Elbogen, Ismar
   1924 *Der jüdische Gottesdienst in seiner geschichtlichen Entwicklung*. Schriften herausgegeben von der Gesellschaft zur Förderung der Wissenschaft des Judentums. Grundriss der Gesamtwissenschaft des Judentums. 2nd revised ed. Frankfurt am Main: J. Kauffmann Verlag.
Evans, Craig A.
   1993 "Mishna and Messiah 'In Context': Some Comments on Jacob Neusner's Proposals." *Journal of Biblical Literature*, 112. Pp. 267-289.
   1995 *Jesus and his Contemporaries*. Arbeiten zur Geschichte des Antiken Judentums und des Urchristentums, 25. Leiden: Brill.
Fiebig, Paul
   1906 *Jesu Blut, ein Geheimnis?* Lebensfragen, Schriften und Reden, 14. Ed. Heinrich Weinel. Tübingen: J.C.B. Mohr.
Flesher, Paul V.M.
   1995 "Rereading the Reredos: David, Orpheus, and Messianism in the Dura Europos Synagogue". *Ancient Synagogues: Historical Analysis and Archaeological Discovery*. Studia Post-Biblica, 47,2. Edited by Dan Urman and Paul V.M. Flesher. Leiden: Brill. Pp. 346-366
Gray, Rebecca
   1993 *Prophetic Figures in late Second Temple Jewish Palestine: The Evidence from Josephus*. Oxford: Oxford University Press.
Gunkel, Hermann
   1903 *Zum religionsgeschichtlichen Verständnis des Neuen Testaments*. Forschungen zur Religion und Literatur des Alten und Neuen Testaments, I. Band 1. Heft. Göttingen: Vandenhoeck & Ruprecht.
   1927 "The 'Historical Movement' in the Study of Religion." *Expository Times* 38 (1926-27). Pp. 532-536 = "Was will die 'religionsgeschichtliche' Bewegung?" *Deutsch-Evangelisch* 5 (1914). Pp. 356ff.
Gutmann, Joseph (ed.)
   1992 *The Dura-Europos Synagogue: A Re-evaluation (1932-1992)*. South-Florida Studies in the History of Judaism, 25. Atlanta, Georgia: Scholars.
Hamman, Adalbert G.
   1987 "Les origines du monachisme chrétien au cours des deux premiers siècles." *Homo Spiritalis: Festgabe für Luc Verheijen Osa zu seinem 70.*

Geburtstag. Ed. Cornelius Mayer with Karl Heinz Chelius. Cassiciacum 38. Würzburg: Augustinus. Pp. 311-326.

Harnack, Adolf
 1900 *Das Wesen des Christentums: Sechzehn Vorlesungen vor Studierenden aller Facultäten im Wintersemester 1899/1900 an der Universität Berlin.* Leipzig: Hinrich. Eng. trans., *What is Christianity? Sixteen Lectures Delivered in the University of Berlin during the Winter Term, 1899-1900.* 3rd rev. ed., London: Williams and Norgate, 1904.

Hart, Henry St John
 1992 "Hosanna in the Highest." *Scottish Journal of Theology* 45 (1992), 283-301.

Hepburn, Ronald W.
 1995 "philosophical practice, the ethics of." *The Oxford Companion to Philosophy.* Ed. Ted Honderich. Oxford/New York: OUP. Pp. 665-666.
 1996 "Landscape and the Metaphyscial Imagination." *Environmental Values* 5. Pp. 191-204.

Hegel, Georg Wilhelm Friedrich
 1807 *Phänomenologie des Geistes.* [750 copies of the 1st. ed. were printed.] Nach dem Texte der Originalausgabe herausgegeben von Johannes Hoffmeister. Der philosophischen Bibliothek Band 114. 6. Auflage. Hamburg: Felix Meiner, 1952.

Héring, Jean
 1958 *La seconde épitre de Saint Paul aux Corinthiens.* Commentaire du Nouveau Testament. Neuchâtel: Delachaux & Niestlé. English translation. *The Second Epistle of Saint Paul to the Corinthians.* London, Epworth Press, 1967.

Hills, Julian V.
 1998 "The Jewish Genius. Jesus according to John Meier." *Forum*, n.s. 1/2. Pp. 327-47.

Holladay, Carl R.
 1989 *Fragments from Hellenistic Jewish Authors.* Vol. II *Poets. The Epic Poets Theodotus and Philo and Ezekiel the Tragedian.* Texts and Translations, 30. Pseudepigrapha Series, 12. Atlanta, Georgia: Scholars Press.

Hollander H.W. and de Jonge, M.
 1985 *The Testaments of the Twelve Patriarchs: A Commentary.* Studia in Veteris Testamenti Pseudepigrapha, 8. Leiden: Brill.

Hopkins, Clark
 1979 *The Discovery of Dura-Europos.* Edited by Bernard Goldman. New Haven and London: Yale University Press.

Horbury, William
 1981 "Suffering and Messianism in Yose ben Yose." *Suffering and Martyrdom in the New Testament: Studies presented to G.M. Styler by the Cambridge New Testament Seminar.* Edited by William Horbury and Brian McNeil. Cambridge: Cambridge University Press. Pp. 143-182.

1985 "The Messianic Association of 'The Son of Man'". *The Journal of Theological Studies* n.s. 36. Pp. 34-55.
1998a *Jewish Messianism and the Cult of Christ*. London: SCM.
1998b *Jews and Christians in Contact and Controversy*. Edinburgh: T&T Clark.

Idelsohn, A.Z
1932 *Jewish Liturgy and its Development*. Cincinnati, Ohio: Holt, Rinehart and Winston, Inc. Reprinted, New York: Schocken Books, 1960.

Jeremias, Joachim
1926 *Golgotha*. Leipzig.
1928 "Die Berufung des Nathanael (Jo 1,45-51)". *Angelos* 3. Pp. 2-5.
1947 *Die Gleichnisse Jesu*. Arbeiten zum Theologie des Alten und Neuen Testaments 11. Zürich: Zwingli-Verlag. 2nd rev. ed., Göttingen: Vandenhoeck & Ruprecht, 1953. 3rd ed., 1954. Final rev. ed., 1965. Eng. trans., *The Parables of Jesus*. London: SCM, 1954. Rev. ed., 1963.

Jülicher, Adolf
1899 *Die Gleichnisreden Jesu. Erster Teil. Die Gleichnisreden Jesu im allgemeinen*. 2. neu bearbeitete Auflage. *Zweiter Teil. Auslegung der Gleichnisreden der drei ersten Evangelien*. Freiburg i. B; Leipzig und Tübingen: J.C.B. Mohr (Paul Siebeck).

Karrer, Martin.
1990 *Der Gesalbte. Die Grundlagen des Christustitels*. Forschungen zur Religion und Literatur des Alten und Neuen Testaments, 151. Göttingen: Vandenhoeck & Ruprecht.

Kraeling, Emil G.
1940 "The Meaning of the Ezekiel Panel in the Synagogue at Dura". *Bulletin of the American Schools of Oriental Research* 78. Pp. 12-18.

Le Déaut, Roger
1963 *La Nuit Pascale: Essai sur la signification de la Pâque juive à partir du Targum d'Exode XII 42*. Analecta Biblica 22. Rome.

Levey, Samson H.
1974 *The Messiah: An Aramaic Interpretation: The Messianic Exegesis of the Targum*. Cincinnati: Hebrew Union College Press.

Lewis, Agnes Smith
1910 *The Old Syriac Gospels or Evangelion Da-Mepharreshê; being the text of the Sinai or Syro-Antiochene Palimpsest, including the latest additions and emendations, with the variants of the Curetonian Text, corroborations from many other MSS., and a list of quotations from ancient authors*. London: Williams and Norgate.
1913 *Light on the Four Gospels from the Sinai Palimpsest*. London: Williams and Norgate.

Lieu, Judith M.
1996 *Image and Reality. The Jews in the World of the Christians in the Second Century*. Edinburgh: T&T Clark.

Lüdemann, Gerd
  1994   *Die Auferstehung Jesu: Historie, Erfahrung, Theologie*. Göttingen: Vandenhoeck & Ruprecht. English translation. *The Resurrection of Jesus: History, Experience, Theology*. London: SCM, 1994.
Luther, Martin
  1532   *Das fünfte, Sechste und Siebende Capitel S. Matthei gepredigt und ausgelegt. Vorrhede D. Mart. Luth. D. Martin Luthers Werke. Kritische Gesamtausgabe*. 32. Band. Weimar: Hermann Böhlaus Nachfolger, 1906. English translation: *Luther's Preface to the Sermon on the Mount. Luther's Works*. Vol. 21. *The Sermon on the Mount (Sermons) and the Magnificat*. Saint Louis: Concordia.
Mack, Burton L.
  1988   *A Myth of Innocence: Mark and Christian Origins*. Philadelphia: Fortress.
  1993   *The Lost Gospel: The Book of Q and Christian Origins*. San Francisco: Harper.
Mackintosh, Hugh Ross
  1937   *Types of Modern Theology. Schleiermacher to Barth*. London: Nisbet and Co. Ltd.
McGinn, Colin
  1991   *The Problem of Consciousness: Essays Towards a Resolution*. Oxford: Blackwell.
Manson, T.W.
  1953   *The Servant-Messiah: A Study in the Public Ministry of Jesus*. Cambridge: Cambridge University Press.
Marcuse, Ludwig
  1959   *Mein zwanzigstes Jahrhundert: Auf dem Weg zu einer Autobiographie*. München.
Meier, John P.
  1991   *A Marginal Jew: Rethinking the Historical Jesus*. Vol. 1. *The Roots of the Problem*. The Anchor Bible Reference Library, New York: Doubleday.
  1994   Vol. 2. *Mentor, Message, and Miracles*.
Moore, George Foot
  1920   Section on "Messiah" in the essay, III Primitive Christianity, essay IV, Christology in *The Beginnings of Christianity Part I The Acts of the Apostles, Vol.I Prologemena I: The Jewish, Gentile and Christian Backgrounds*. Edited by F.J. Foakes Jackson and Kirsopp Lake. London: Macmillan and Co., Limited. The Editors were responsible for the essay, Christology, pp. 345-418, and Moore wrote, at their behest, the section on pp. 346-362.
Moule, C.F.D.
  1977   *The Origin of* Christology. Cambridge: Cambridge University Press.

Nagel, Ernest and Newman, James R.
- 1959 *Gödel's Proof.* London: Routledge and Kegan Paul. Paperback ed. 1971.

Neusner, Jacob
- 1984 *Messiah in Context: Israel's History and Destiny in Formative Judaism.* Studies in Judaism. Lanham MD: University Press of America. Repr. 1988.
- 1987 *Judaisms and Their Messiahs at the Turn of the Christian Era.* Edited by Jacob Neusner, William Scott Green and Ernest S. Frerichs. Cambridge: Cambridge University Press.
- 1993 "The Mishna in Philosophical Context and out of Canonical Bounds" [a reply to Craig A. Evans]. *Journal of Biblical Literature*, 112. Pp. 291-304.

Oegema, Gerbern S.
- 1994 *Der Gesalbte und sein Volk: Untersuchungen zum Konzeptualisierungsprozess der messianischen Erwartungen von den Makkabäern bis Bar Koziba.* Schriften des Institutum Judaicum Delitzschianum 2. Göttingen: Vandenhoeck & Ruprecht. English translation: *The Anointed and his People: Messianic Expectations from the Maccabees to Bar Kochba.* JSP Supplement Series 27. Sheffield: Sheffield Academic Press, 1998.

Ogden, Schubert M.
- 1961 *Christ without Myth: A study based on the theology of Rudolf Bultmann.* British edition: London: Collins, 1962.
- 1982 *The Point of Christology: The 1980 Sarum Lectures.* London: SCM.

O'Neill, J.C.
- 1968-69 "The Silence of Jesus." *New Testament Studies* 15 (1968-69). Pp. 153-167
- 1970 "The Charge of Blasphemy at Jesus' Trial before the Sanhedrin." *The Trial of Jesus: Cambridge Studies in Honour of C.F.D.Moule*, ed. Ernst Bammel. London: SCM. Pp. 72-77.
- 1979 "The Lamb of God in the Testaments of the Twelve Patriarchs". *Journal for the Study of the New Testament*, 2. Pp. 2-30. Reprinted with corrections in *New Testament Background Reader*, edited by Stanley Porter and Craig Evans. Sheffield: Sheffield Academic Press, 1997.
- 1980a *Messiah: Six lectures on the ministry of Jesus.* Cambridge: Cochrane Press. Repr. 1984.
- 1980b "Can we avoid the conclusion that God exists?" *The Philosopher* 18 no. 2. Pp. 15-20.
- 1981 "Did Jesus teach that his death would be vicarious as well as typical?" *Suffering and Martyrdom in the New Testament: Studies presented to G.M. Styler by the Cambridge New Testament Seminar.* Edited by William Horbury and Brian McNeil. Cambridge: Cambridge University Press. Pp. 9-27.

1983 "The *Unforgivable* Sin." *Journal for the Study of the New Testament* 19. Essays in Honour of E. Bammel. Edited by William Horbury and Christopher Rowland. Pp. 37-42.

1988 "The Source of the Parables of the Bridegroom and the Wicked Husbandmen." *The Journal of Theological Studies* new series 39. Pp. 485-489.

1989a "The Origins of Monasticism." *The Making of Orthodoxy: Essays in Honour of Henry Chadwick.* Ed. Rowan Williams. Cambridge: Cambridge University Press. Pp. 270-287.

1989b "The Rules Followed by the Editors of the Text Found in the Codex Vaticanus." *New Testament Studies* 35. Pp. 219-228.

1991a "The Man from Heaven: *SibOr* 5.256-259." *Journal for the Study of the Pseudepigrapha* 9. Pp. 87-102.

1991b "The Desolate House and the New Kingdom of Jerusalem: Jewish Oracles of Ezra in 2 Esdras 1-2." *Templum Amicitiae: Essays on the Second Temple presented to Ernst Bammel.* Journal for the Study of the New Testament Supplement Series, 48. Edited by William Horbury. Sheffield: Sheffield Academic Press. Pp. 226-236.

1993a Review of Reiser. *The Journal of Theological Studies,* n.s. 44. Pp. 228-235.

1993b "The Kingdom of God." *Novum Testamentum* 35. Pp. 130-141.

1994a "The Question of Messianic Expectation in Pseudo-Philo's Biblical Antiquities." *The Journal of Higher Criticism,* 1. Pp. 85-93.

1994b "What is Joseph and Aseneth about?" *Henoch* 16. Pp. 189-198.

1995 *Who Did Jesus Think He Was?* Biblical Interpretation Series, 11. Leiden: Brill.

1997a "A Vision for the Church: John's Gospel." *A Vision for the Church: Studies in Early Christian Ecclesiology in Honour of J.P.M. Sweet.* Ed. Markus Bockmuehl and Michael B. Thompson. Edinburgh: T&T Clark. Pp. 79-93.

1997b "The Shocking Prospect of Killing the Messiah (Luke 20:9-19)." *Jesus and His Parables: Interpreting the Parables of Jesus Today.* Ed. V. George Shillington. Edinburgh: T&T Clark. Pp. 165-176.

1998 "New Testament Monasteries." *Common Life in the Early Church: Essays Honoring Graydon F. Snyder.* Ed. Julian V. Hills with Richard B. Gardner, Robert Jewett, Robert Neff, Peter Richardson, David M. Scholer, and Virginia Wiles. Harrisburg, Pennsylvania: Trinity Press International. Pp. 118-132.

1999 "Jesus of Nazareth." *The Journal of Theological Studies,* n.s. 50. Pp. 135-42.

Pascal, Blaise

1962 *Pensées. Texte établi par Louis Lafuma. Préface d'André Dodin.* Livre de Vie, 24. Paris: Éditions du Seuil. *Pensées.* Everyman's Library, 874. Translated by W.F. Trotter. Introduction by T.S. Eliot. London: Dent, 1932.

Pomykala, Kenneth E.
- 1995 *The Davidic Dynasty Tradition in Early Judaism. Its History and Significance for Messianism*. Society of Biblical Literature: Early Judaism and its Literature, 7. Atlanta, Georgia: Scholars Press.

Priest, Stephen
- 1990 *The British Empiricists: Hobbes to Ayer*. London: Penguin.

Ramsey, Frank Plumpton
- 1931 *The Foundation of Mathematics and other Logical Essays*. Ed. R.B. Braithwaite. London. Pp. 206-211

Reiser, Marius
- 1990 *Die Gerichtspredigt Jesu. Eine Untersuchung zur eschatologischen Verkündigung Jesu und ihrem frühjüdischen Hintergrund*. Neutestamentliche Abhandlungen, Neue Folge 23. Münster: Aschendorff.

Riches, John
- 1980 *Jesus and the Transformation of Judaism*. London: Darton, Longman and Todd.

Sanders, E.P.
- 1977 *Paul and Palestinian Judaism: A Comparison of Patterns of Religion*. London: SCM.
- 1983 *Paul, the Law, and the Jewish People*. Philadelphia: Fortress.
- 1992 *Judaism: Practice and Belief 63 BCE–66 CE*. London: SCM.

Schechter, Solomon
- 1909 *Some Aspects of Rabbinic Theology*. London: Adam and Charles Black. Reprinted as *Aspects of Rabbinic Theology*. Woodstock: Jewish Lights, 1993.

Schleiermacher, Friedrich
- 1830 *Der christliche Glaube nach den Grundsätzen der evangelischen Kirche im Zusammenhang dargestellt*. Two vols. 2nd ed. English trans. *The Christian Faith*. Ed. H.R. Mackintosh and J.S. Stewart. Edinburgh: T. & T. Clark, 1938.

Schuller, Eileen
- 1990 "4Q372 1: A Text about Joseph". *Revue de Qumran* 14 (1989-90). Pp. 349-376.

Schürer, Emil
- 1973-87 *The History of the Jewish People in the Age of Jesus Christ (175 B.C.–A.D. 135). A New English Version*. Literary editor, Pamela Vermes; organizing editor, Matthew Black. Vol. 1 revised and edited by Geza Vermes and Fergus Millar. Edinburgh: T&T Clark, 1973. Vol. 2, revised and edited by Geza Vermes, Fergus Millar, Matthew Black, 1979. Vol. 3, revised and edited by Geza Vermes, Fergus Millar, Martin Goodman. Part 1, 1986; Part 2, 1987.

Schüssler Fiorenza, Elisabeth
- 1983 *In Memory of Her: A Feminist Theological Reconstruction of Christian Origins*. New York: Crossroad.

Segal, Alan F.
  1996 "The Akedah: Some Reconsiderations". *Geschichte—Tradition—Reflexion: Festschrift für Martin Hengel zum 70.Geburtstag.* Vol. I. *Judentum.* Edited by Peter Schäfer. Tübingen: J.C.B. Mohr (Paul Siebeck). Pp. 99-116.

Singer, S
  1962 *The Authorised Daily Prayer Book of the United Hebrew Congregations of the British Commonwealth of Nations.* Published under the sanction of Chief Rabbi Dr Nathan Marcus Adler. New edition reset and enlarged under the direction of Israel Brodie, Chief Rabbi. London: Eyre and Spottiswoode.

Smith, B.T.D.
  1937 *The Parables of the Synoptic Gospels: A Critical Study.* Cambridge: University Press.

Smith, Norman Kemp
  1935 *Hume's Dialogues Concerning Natural Religion.* Oxford: Clarendon Press. 2nd ed., with supplement, New York: Social Sciences, 1948.

Smith, Morton
  1959 "What is implied by the variety of messianic figures?" *Journal of Biblical Literature* 78. Pp. 66-72.

Sprigge, T.L.S.
  1993 *James and Bradley: American Truth and British Reality.* Chicago and La Salle, Illinois: Open Court.

Sukenik, E.L.
  1934 *Ancient Synagogues in Palestine and Greece.* The Schweich Lectures, 1930. London: For the British Academy, Humphrey Milford Oxford University Press.

Traub, W.
  1954 οὐρανός &c. *Theologisches Wörterbuch zum Neuen Testament.* 5. Band. Stuttgart: Kohlhammer. Pp. 496-501; 509-543. *Theological Dictionary of the New Testament.* Vol. V. Grand Rapids, Michigan: Eerdmans, 1967. Pp. 497-502; 509-543.

Trompf, Johannes
  1993 *The Assumption of Moses: A Critical Edition with Commentary.* Studia in Veteris Testamenti Pseudepigrapha, 10. Leiden: Brill.

Vermes, Geza
  1961 *Scripture and Tradition in Judaism: Haggadic Studies.* Studia Post-Biblica, 4. Leiden: Brill. "Redemption and Genesis xxii—The Binding of Isaac and the Sacrifice of Jesus." Pp. 193-227.
  1973 *Jesus the Jew: A historian's reading of the Gospels.* London: Collins.
  1995 *The Dead Sea Scrolls in English.* 4th ed., London: Penguin.

Wells, G.A.
  1975 *Did Jesus Exist?* London: Elek/Pemberton. 2nd revised ed. Pemberton, 1986.

Westcott, Brooke Foss
- 1866 *The Gospel of the Resurrection*. London: Macmillan. 3rd ed., 1874.

Williams, Bernard
- 1995 *Making Sense of Humanity and Other Philosophical Papers 1982–1993*. Cambridge: Cambridge University Press.
- 1996 "On Hating and Despising Philosophy." *London Review of Books*, 18 April 1996. Pp. 17-18.

Wischnitzer, Rachel
- 1948 *The Messianic Theme in the Paintings of the Dura Synagogue*. Chicago: University of Chicago Press.

Wiseman, T.P.
- 1987 "'There went out a decree from Caesar Augustus...'" *New Testament Studies* 33. Pp. 479-480.

Wollheim, Richard
- 1963 *Hume on Religion: Selected and Introduced by Richard Wollheim*. Fontana Library: Theology and Philosophy. London: Collins.